I0439705

# Goodbye; Between Us Only!

# They Will Not Publish This!

## By Majid Al Suleimany

**My Books Websites –**

www.myownmajid.com

www.myown-ebooks.com

www.majidbooks.com

**My Columns**

www.majidwritecom

www.majidall.com

**November 29, 2014**

**To Order This Book Directly: -**

www.createspace.com/5139836

**Recommended that this book to be read together with: -**

Writing: My Passion! – www.createspace.com/5085322

# I    PREFACE

**This book is the 10<sup>th</sup> book in The Series - Between Us Only! And my 20<sup>th</sup> book so far.**

In order to expedite the book publishing process, minimal images are going to be inserted.

Paramount importance is to get all my articles Post last Between Us Only1 series – Wipe My Tears! The book was published in June 2013 – all intended to put all my books in one place for further references and for record purposes!

I have also included all those articles after end of my columns mainly based on 'a Technicality' designed to stop and to end my columns.

I was keeping to myself and trying to avoid conflict – but still people were after me! So I decided to accept the challenge – and write and record this book as last of my columns writings for future records and references.

No one can kill the soul and heart of a Writer – because so long as a Writer will live he will not stop writing!

As Jules Renard had said – No one considers a Writer as ridiculous – even if he does not make any money! So there! Besides, I had posted this in all The Social Media - November 13, 2014

- **One - Do you watch the News? – www.myownmajid.com – Speak The Truth Always!**

Why are we so set against each other? We will support The Foreigner and The Expatriate but not esteem and value our own! We do not have trust and confidence on our own! It is part of this great CURSE Jealousy, Envy and Bad Hearts within us! Bad unfeeling uncaring hearts inside some of us only! Pure evil-like just as is ISIS!

- **Two - I met some guys who were trying to tell me that 'there were some typos' in The Arabic – Behind The Wheel!**

This is not true! The book was translated by Experts and also Proof Read too by others!

We must stop these vile silly games to hurt one another! If you do not want to help or support someone – just tell him face to face vis-à-vis that I can help you with 'a lift of my phone – but chose not to!' Better that so we move along.

- **Three - Do you watch the news – www.myownmajid.com – Speak The Truth Always!**

One Top Big Bank supports all Indian etc. functions in Oman. 4 times I have gone to them – and they have turned down me flat! Some even give my books to THEIR EXPERTS to Review – and they are all Expatriates Residents and Foreigners! None of them will support my books – because I call A Spade A Spade – and always Speak The Truth – which they Do Not Want! This is A Road Safety Book – Why hurt it – when Statistics prove that The Society Really Needs This Book For Safer Driving! Especially The Youth!

**Take Care! Allah God Protect and Preserve us All! Ameen Amen**

**Majid Al Suleimany**
**The Author**
**November 28, 2014**

**II          All Majid Al Suleimany Books (19).**
**This one 20ᵗʰ!**
### The Arab Management Books (4).

| Psychology of Arab Management Thinking! | www.trafford.com/08-0889 |
|---|---|
| Arab Management: Reality or Myth? | www.createspace.com/4960056 |
| ** The Arab Manager! The Call! | www.createspace.com/5083875 |
| ** A Cry For Help! | http://bookstore.trafford.com/Products/SKU-000142695/A-Cry-For-Help.aspx |
| ** Twin Versions | |

## The Road Safety Books (3)!

| Being The Safe Driver! | www.createspace.com/4097374 |
|---|---|
| Behind The Wheel! | www.createspace.com/4655681 |
| Arabic – Behind The Wheel! | www.createspace.com/4875352 |
| My Books Websites – www.myownmajid.com – www.myown-ebookscom<br><br>Road Safety – www.bethesafedrivercom | |
| | |

**All About My Books (3)!**

| ** Writing: My Passion! | www.createspace.com/5085322 |
|---|---|
| ** All About My Books! | www.createspace.com/5071159 |
| ** What They Said About My Books! | www.createspace.com/5026372 |

| ** Same Versions |
|---|
| My Books Websites – www.myownmajid.com – www.myown-ebookscom |
| http://myownmajid.com/2014/11/08/all-about-my-19-books-to-date/ |

## Between Us Only! Series Books (10)!

| The Final Touchdown! | www.createspace.com/5026372 |
|---|---|
| Wipe My Tears! | www.createspace.com/4304972 |
| The Sequel – 3! | www.createspace.com/4153263 |
| Short Takes – 2! | www.createspace.com/41532639 |

## Between Us Only! Series Books!

| | |
|---|---|
| **The Sequel!** | **www.trafford.com/08-0890** |
| **Short Takes!** | **ID 1000241739 – www.createspace.com** |
| **My Books Websites – www.myownmajid.com – www.myown-ebookscom** | |

## Between Us Only! Series Books!

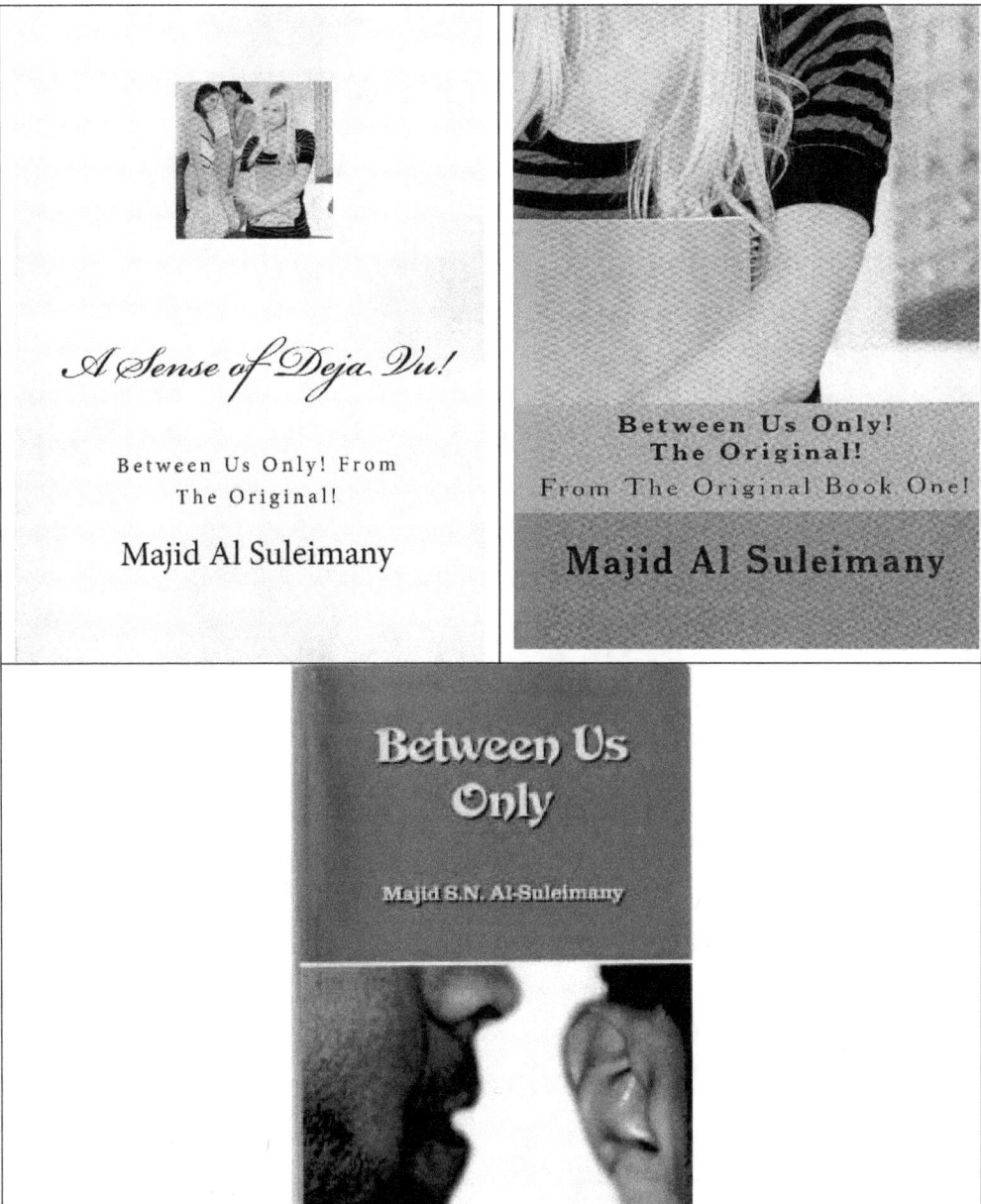

| ** A Sense of Déjà vu! | www.createspace.com/5060552 |
|---|---|
| ** Between Us Only! The Original! (Redo!) | www.createspace.com/5041985 |
| ** Between Us Only! The First Book! | www.myownmajid.com |
| My Books Websites – www.myownmajid.com – www.myown-ebookscom | |
| ** Same Versions<br>November 8, 2014 | |

And this one 10th Book in Between Us Only! Series – They Will Not Publish This!

The Author
November 28, 2014

# III   Copyrights

## © Copyrights - Majid Al Suleimany

Applicable copyrights of The Sultanate of Oman (OM) and wherever the book will be published with The Author's written consent.

All rights reserved. No part of this publication may be reproduced, stored in a retrieval system, or transmitted, in any form or by any means, electronic, mechanical, photocopying, recording or otherwise, without the written permission of The Author.

In case of any violations, Legal Action will be taken to ensure such Copyrights – as stipulated above.

The Images used in this book are from **www.istockphoto.com** - **www.shutterstock.com** and mainly from **www.majidall.com** .

Also from **www.theomanobserver.om** – where the Author is a Columnist with 3 columns. Especially Between Us Only! –search under Google.

The cover image comes from **www.istockphoto.com** and the cover has been designed by Artist Raadheesh Krishna. Some of his caricatures have also been used in the book.

**In addition to this book - going into production at the same time - are the Author's New Books: -**

- **Behind The Wheel! – The Road Safety Book**
- **Between Us Only! – Short Takes – The Sequel – Two!**
- **Between Us Only! – The Sequel! – Three!**
- **Details and Information at**
- **www.myown-ebooks.com**
- **www.myownmajid.com**
- **www.majidbooks.com**
- **www.bethesafedriver.com**

**Between Us Only! Images - www.istockphoto.com**

# IV        List of Contents

**Note: - This Book Should Be Read Together With This One Below –**

# A.01.      About The Book!

## Goodbye; Between Us Only! They Will Not Publish This!

Back again for the next installment in his critically acclaimed series, The Author offers a new collection of articles that deal with the delicate matters that many are scared to touch.

Adapted from his successful newspaper column in *The Oman Daily Observer*, the enlightening and educational articles of *Goodbye; Between Us Only! They Will Not Publish This!* The book covers everything from human suffering and social trends to divorce and prejudice.

Touching on some of the social evils prevalent in today's society, this fantastic collection uses a mixture of witty observations and heavy blows to get its point across. A labor of love filled with keen observations on twenty-first-century society, this insightful book carries priceless warnings, resentments, fears, and advice for readers everywhere.

The varied and honest new collection of articles cover a multitude of topics, from lighthearted and entertaining stories to serious topics based off of universal societal issues. Full of interesting and educational articles and stories, this wonderful book is a captivating experience, especially for readers familiar with Arab customs, traditions, heritages, and legacies.

A fantastic read for everyone from CEOs to students - *Goodbye; Between Us Only! They Will Not Publish This!* The book does offer insightful and illuminating articles based off of a variety of topics that even apply to children, teenagers, and grandparents. Filled with varied topics that will entertain and inform readers of all backgrounds and walks of life, this eclectic collection will engross as it inspires and provides a wide range of knowledge on a multitude of important topics.

Developed from weekly columns the Author writes - *Goodbye; Between Us Only! They Will Not Publish This!* The book follows up on the success of the previous books in the series and furthers the idea of private talks between friends on matters that many are too scared to touch. Often times delving into topics that aren't always sweet, this enlightening book uses a clear and elegant prose to explore social evils in society as well as their lighthearted counterparts.

Covering a variety of priceless topics, this wonderful collection of articles gives readers everywhere a glimpse into the issues that are prevalent in today's society.

## Back Cover Text

Back again for the next installment in his critically acclaimed series, The Author offers a new collection of articles that deal with the delicate matters that many are scared to touch. Adapted from his successful newspaper column in *The Oman Daily Observer*, these enlightening and educational articles cover everything from human suffering and social trends to divorce and prejudice.

Touching on some of the social evils prevalent in today's society, this fantastic collection uses a mixture of witty observations and heavy blows to get its point across.

A labor of love filled with keen observations on twenty-first-century society, this insightful book carries priceless warnings, resentments, fears, and advice for readers everywhere.

The Author has over twenty-five years of experience as a human resources specialist and over ten years of experience as a management and human resources consultant, expert, and advisor.

For the past eight years, he has written weekly columns in *The Oman Daily Observer!* - An English daily, which has led to three published books based off of his columns. He has recently expanded to a new column with entitled - At the Workplace.

The Author has also published four other books on Arab Management. He began writing at age fourteen and has since developed a new approach that he feels is "direct from the heart."

The Author holds a MBA in International Management (UK). For more information on him, please visit **www.myownmajid.com** - **www.myown-ebooks.com** and **www.majidbooks.com**.

### *Goodbye; Between Us Only! They Will Not Publish This!*

# A.02        The Author Biography

The Author has over twenty-five years of experience as a human resources specialist and over ten years of experience as a management and human resources consultant, expert, and advisor.

For the past eight years, he has written weekly columns in *The Oman Daily Observer*, an English daily, which has led to three published books based off of his columns. He has recently expanded to a new column with entitled, At the Workplace.

The Author has also published four other books on Arab Management. A new book on Road Safety titled Being The Safe Driver! Behind The Wheel! **www.bethesafedriver.com** He began writing at age fourteen and has since developed a new approach that he feels is "direct from the heart." Al Suleimany holds a MBA in International Management (UK).

He is married and has three daughters and a son. And 4 grandchildren.

For more information on him, please visit **www.myown-ebooks.com** – **www.myownmajid.com** and **www.majidbooks.com**.

In addition to this book, there are also – Short Takes – Between Us Only! - and The Sequel – Between Us Only – Book Two – from my First Book of the same name – Between Us Only! – Book One.

The books contain series of articles that had appeared during the last five years in The Oman Daily Observer (English Daily). The subjects cover varies from week to week but range from Socio-political, Social, Economic, Family, Educational, Omanisation (Localisation), Management, Human Resources, Training & Development, International arena and scenarios etc.

Amongst the famous widely acclaimed read articles in **Book One - Between Us Only** are – Burning Homes; Advice To A New CEO; The Land Rover Story; The Power Of The Media; The Humane Face Amongst War; Are You Afraid?; What Is Happening To Us Now?; Keeping Up With The Changes; How Much Dowry For Your Daughter; Do Not Be Worry – Be Happy; There Is No Urgency.

**Also -**  Learning To Say No; Soul-Searching and Self-Analysis; No Money No Honey; Decision Making; Tragic Love Story; Why we Lie and Cheat; Why Are We So Bad?; and How To Apply For A Job?- varied articles for different tastes and likes – covering almost everyone – from the Student to the CEO, from the child, teenager to Grand Parents!

This book contains equally interesting subjects and topics. These are articles after my first two books in the series – and the original Book one of the same name

Though some of them have been made out as stories, but the messages coming out are openly vividly and crystal clear to all, in many cases tit comes out outright and facing the Reader without any doubt or innuendos.

When I had previously had asked The Editor of The Oman Daily Observer - on what articles to produce in this Book – he said to me – **All of Them.** That is the best compliment any Author can get!

The articles in this book appear from May 2013 onwards – and that have appeared in my two columns in The Oman Daily Observer – Between Us Only! And At My Workplace!

More information and details in my book sites at **www.myown-ebooks.com** and **www.majidbooks.com Also new one www.myownmajid.com**

**Between Us Only!**

**Images - www.istockphoto.com**

# A.03.       Contact Addresses

## My Postal Address

**Post Office Box 230 – Mina Al Fahal – Muscat – Sultanate of Oman – Postal Code 116.**

## My Websites

**For This Book Especially: -**
**www.myown-ebooks.com**
**www.bethesafedriver.com**
**www.majidbooks.com**
**www.myownmajid.com**
**www.majidalsuleimany.com**

## Others: -

**www.majidsuleimany.com**
**www.mas-trac.com**
**www.alsuleimany.com**
**www.majidall.com**
**www.majidsn.com**
**www.betweenusonly.com**

## My E-Mails

**majidalsuleimanybooks@gmail.com**
**majid@majidalsuleimany.com**
**majidsnalsuleimany@hotmail.com**
**majidalsuleimany@gmail.com**
**majidalsuleimany@yahoo.com**
**majid@mas-trac.com**
**majid@majidsuleimany.com**

## Residence

**Way 1028 – Villa 1099**
**Qurum Heights (PDO)**

## Mobile / GSM

**+968 (Oman Code)**
**95207511**
**95116953**

**November 28, 2014**

Between Us Only!  - www.istockphoto.com

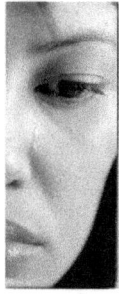

**Wipe My Tears!  – www.majidall.com**

# A.04.        Dedications  & Indebtedness

**To: -**

My Late Parents – Peace Be Upon Them
All My Family - My Wife (Safiya / Rashda),
My Children (Twin Girls – Majda and Maliha, Son Fahad and Daughter Marwa) and
My granddaughters - (Aliyazah, Maria, Ritaal and Sibel),
My son-in-laws Ali and Saleh and Suhaib.
My daughter-in-law Tabinda
My Late Mother-in-law - PBUH - who had always prayed for me till her last breath on earth

**And also to:-**

All the Al Suleimany Family - my Brothers, my Sisters, their children, their families and related.

**And To All My Fans, Readers and Supporters**.

**The Author**

**Muscat – Sultanate of Oman –**

**November 28, 2014**

Between Us Only!

Images - www.istockphoto.com

More information and details in my book sites at www.myownmajid.com - www.myown-ebooks.com and www.majidbooks.com

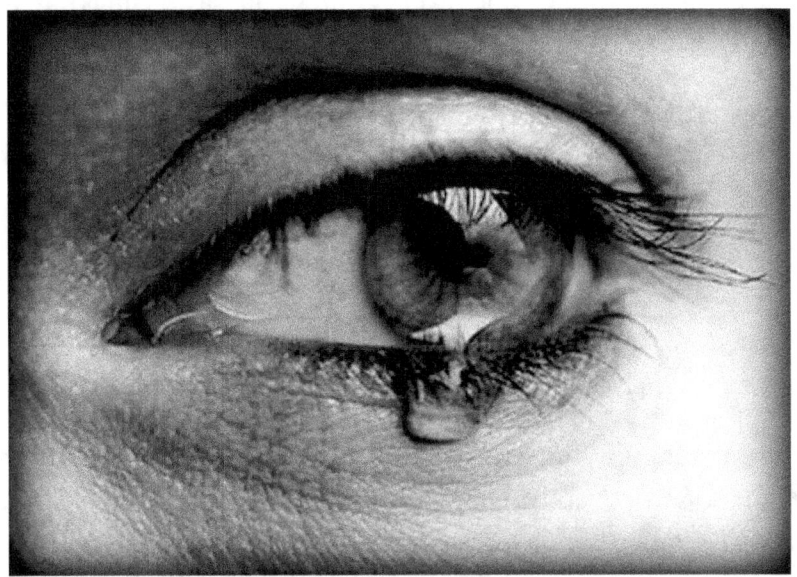

**Wipe My  Tears! - www.majidall.com**

## A.05        New Comments from the Readers –

- I read your article and I must say, it was an eye opener for me - **Omani HR Executive**

- You said it so beautifully my dear that my heart broke out for you. I cry in my heart for you. You are so great**! - From A Lady Fan (Omani**

- What a brilliant article, I wish I had joined the book group sooner – **British Fan**

- Do men read your articles? They are the usual main culprits! I love it. Thanks - **From A Lady Fan (Omani)**

- It was nice to see that you have compiled all your articles in your books to be reserved for future generations – **Local Great Literary person**

- People respect you as our number one Columnist and for the wonderful pieces you have said over the number of years. It is our great pleasure and we are proud to have such quality Omani columnists like yourself on our side – **Senior Omani Journalist**

- You really talk deeply and with great understanding to human nature. You are lucky to be you! – and every word you say is making great sense.– **Omani IT Head**

- This was the best lot so far – **IT Specialist (Indian)**

- Thanks brother for your truthful and honest commentary – and all that you had said are very true and wonderful too - but this is the best one! – **A Family Member.**

- Your columns are an inspiration to all aspiring young Omani journalists and writers in English language – **Senior Indian Journalist.**

- You are among the few who are visionary and with realistic foresight. You have mentioned exactly what the mindset of our young Omanis think – **Senior IT Consultant (Omani)**

- You are truly one of the few peoples that one can easily connect with. It is always easier to be behind the scenes - than it is to be in the frontline. Only few can be like you! – **Young Omani Fan (Lady)**

- Thank you greatly! You enrich us always with your articles and contributions. I also do appreciate your ideas and suggestions – highly remarkable and commendable always! - **Omani IT Head**

- One thing for sure that you often get us some lovely and valued real stories which exposes wisdom to enlighten our lives. I thank you a lot for your contribution to educate the society, whether directly or indirectly – **Omani CEO.**

- Truthfully you are in an enviable position where some may resent your views and outlooks – but there is nothing that they can do to you adversely because you are out in the open for all to see – and this plane has already taken off from the ground – **Literary Person (Indian).**

- Indeed, I doubt if we will ever see (in my life time) another person like you with such these qualities – **Omani Senior Engineer.**

- I have been blessed to work with great people like you – and I always remember the pleasure of working with you when you were with us – **British CEO.**

- *The true value of gold is only known by the goldsmiths and people who knows what exactly gold means* – **Omani Artist**

- The day you left us – the before stale air blew over us in the Company once again – **British GM**

- It was nice to see that you have compiled all your articles in your books to be reserved for future generations – **from a Local Great Literary person (Omani)**

- Great experience and thoughts. We need more people like you in spreading such thoughts and standing on Change – **Omani Engineering Head**

- You really talk deeply and with great understanding to human nature. You are lucky to be you! – and every word you say is making great sense. only – **Omani IT Head**

- Great experience and thoughts. We need more people like you spreading such thoughts and standing on Change – **Omani Senior Engineer**

- It was nice to see that you have compiled all your articles in your books to be reserved for future generations – **from a Local Great Literary person**

- The University expresses its many thanks for being in touch - and is a huge pleasure and privilege and a great honour. You have a brilliant and star colossal range of achievements - and must be congratulated – **UK University Professor**

- The best part I mostly enjoy is that you write from the bottom of your heart. Your writing skills are really excellent! – **Senior Public Official**

- Your contributions to the good of society and especially The Youth can never be marginalised or ignored – **Another Senior Public Official**

- **More comments and remarks at www.myown-ebooks.com and www.myownmajid.com**

**Between Us Only! - The Secret!**

**Images - www.istockphoto.com**

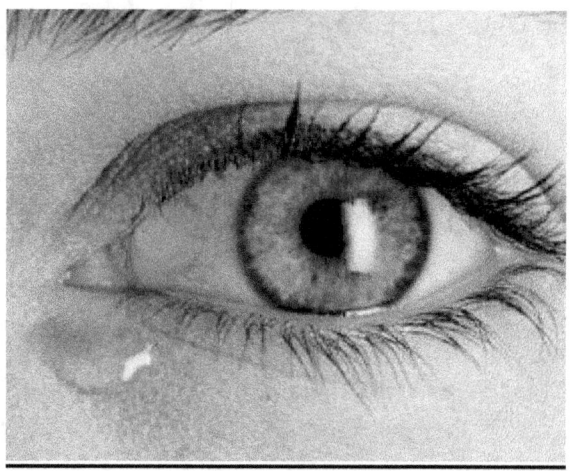

**Wipe My Tears!**

**Image Tears – www.majidall.com**

Between Us Only! Images - www.istockphoto.com

Wipe My Tears! – www.majidall.com

## A.06 - Book One –
## Between Us Only Reviews!

**An author in search of values and ethics - Oman Daily Observer – Features Editor (TT Joseph).**

**September 10 2005**
**Press Coverage - Between Us Only!**

*by Majid Said Nasser Al Suleimany*
*434 pages, Price RO 9*

*Available at Family Bookshop Turtle Bookshops  and all*
*leading bookshops in Oman /  Magrudy in UAE*

Majid Al Suleimany is a well-read, witty and prolific writer who often makes you laugh and sit up and think on ordinary but often neglected and not so cared matters in the society. He also writes about social evils prevalent in the society with a funny touch and lashes it with heavy blows.

This unique style and way we rarely find in other writers. His prose is simple and clear and elegant.

The collection of his columns published in the Observer and some unpublished ones appear in a book form — Between Us Only.

The title itself tells the reader the topics he talks about are not so sweet many times, and many of the articles irritate somebody or other.

Since it is 'between us only' and whispered in to your ears he often talks about matters which many are scared to touch. He talks about burning homes, divorce, pride and prejudice, human suffering, human fears, social trends and changes and people's idiotic concerns to keep up with the Joneses.

As a human resources professional, in his essays Majid gives very important and valuable tips and notes to company executives and chiefs.

Looking at the society's craze for materialism and vanity the writer asks: "What happened to the sanctity of marriage as the highest institution in our lives according to our Islamic teachings — the Sunnah and the Hadith? Our customs, traditions and heritage?"

Divorces are happening at the drop of a hat. So he advises "we need to impart to our younger generations the sanctity and high importance of the institution of marriage. The importance of patience, harmony, tolerance, trust, faith, and confidence. This is in order to save our society for future generations."

In an advice to chief executive officers and managers the author reminds "what happened to all the principles of treating staff with respect, with utmost ethics, professionalism, kindness, cordial reception and courtesy? Whether they are Omanis or others, people need to be treated properly and with more esteem and respect."

As a Human Resources Consultant, Majid is giving valuable tips to job applicants in his article "Applying for a job". Some very important dos and don'ts for the aspiring job seekers. "Send your application with jus Photostat copies of your certificates and other documents.

"When you are called for an interview do not tremble and show fear and worries. Remain cool, collected, calm and in control. "Never ask 'how much you will pay me' until an offer has actually been made. "Prepare your CV (maximum two typed pages only) and a covering letter (one page only) with your application.

In another article he asks: "What is this new ugly and unpleasant developments now in our homes? This 'domestic violence' thing? Do we have an excuse for this?

The satellite dishes, and the foreign films and dramas that are beamed to our homes? Or is that the new in-thing fashion now, the provocations and 'do not care stuff' — followed by lifting of hand and beating out that poor creature that bore you babies that you call your own and have made you proud too?

Do you consider the effect on the children? Hey, what is wrong with us nowadays?"

Majid's "Between us Only" is a sincere attempt by a simple human being who cherishes his culture and traditions, and wanted it to be preserved for the coming generations. It is a labour of love with keen observation of the society in the 21st century Arab world in particular. It also carries warnings, resentments, and fears and advises for all.

**Between Us Only! The Secret! Images - www.istockphoto.com**

**More information and details in my book sites at www.myown-ebooks.com and www.majidbooks.com**

**Also new one at www.myownmajid.com**

**Wipe My Tears! – www.majidall.com**

# A.07    Comments & Readers' Comments – Book One.

- The writer takes 'a no hold approach' in many of his writings with an outlook from a personal perspective, example and experiences.

- You will find that you will want to read ALL of them, once you reach the end!

- Hello Majid - If we don't comment on what you are writing it doesn't mean we don't appreciate, no, me my self I believe and enjoy every word you write. The incidents you are talking about have occurred in front of our eyes and have seen people suffer for what they have done. But Majid do people learn from that?. Everyone says "he is stupid. It will never happen to me. If I were him I would...." and they continue with the same what others have suffered from.

- Yesterday I watched Oprah show  and she explained that it is the brain that makes people act the way they act in spite of seeing it is wrong. I'm confused Majid how can we help people we love and surrounding us into seeing things differently? Does power and money change people attitudes or they just unveils them to show their original beings?

Do write we will read. Thanks for forwarding me the nice pieces. I enjoy them. Good bless you – Omani Lady Fan

- The writer takes 'a no hold approach' in many of his writings with an outlook from a personal perspective, fresh and in a retrospective view and in examples and experiences – something new and refreshing in Oman (please do not quote my name in the feedback)" - Head of Human Resources and Development (Large Company - Omani).

- Where do you get the guts to write such stuff? Please do not quote me!' **Many**

- What you say many of us want to say too, but in our hearts only. You see we lack the guts! – Omani Human Resources Professional (Retired).

- Let us put it this way. Most of your articles are cautionary and advisory; they expect to sell well. Take it from me and from X – CEO Omani Banker – Indian Senior Banker.

- You are the greatest – British Fan (Military Officer)

- I like most that article about being yourself  – **Indian – Teacher (English)**

- How many hits did you get in your *website (**www.alsuleimany.com**). You know there is a way of finding out! – **Company Owner and Executive President**

- The man has brains, and he shows it too! – **Omani Accountant**

- Don't talk to him, he will quote you in his next column! – **A Director – Oil Company.**

- I take your articles to read at home when I want to unwind and relax; I simply have no time in the Office nowadays! – Indian GM.

- I find that I will want to read it all over again, that is why I take it home to read it in the lunch break – Senior Finance Accountant - Indian

- We better be nice about you, before you write on us – Finance Accountant (Indian)

- I feel that it feels great to read his human interest stories … The facts, which were objectively outlined, need to be studied in finding a solution to the many problems that haunt families today …must have made a lot of families think twice before getting into certain troubles that lead to disaster …. Such human-interest articles are exactly what we readers are patiently waiting for. Carry on the good works – **by Omani Lady – Muscat – Letters to the Editor – Oman Daily Observer – 15th August, 2003.**

- I enjoy reading your article every week - **Omani Doctor.**

- You made my day! – **Senior Omani Banker**

- I have now become a great fan of yours! – **Indian Lady**

- I see you every Wednesday and say Hello to you – but you do not see me!. I never miss reading your very good articles – **Omani Head Relations – Representative Office in Oman.**

- I read your article, and it made me real cry. I gave it to the wife, and she too cried with me. Thank you! We both needed that cry to unwind! Now there is love in the air! (please do not use my name – **CEO (Indian).**

- I have real enjoyed reading your article. In giving your personal examples and examples, we seem to know you more and more day by day – **Omani Senior Engineer**

- Last week I was overseas on Official business and missed your article. Can you send me a copy or E-Mail me, please – **Senior Public Official.**

- If you know who reads your articles, you will faint – **as above.**

- I do not want to give you a big head, but yes, I do read your articles – they are very good, insightful and comes with a fresh air, nothing we are used too here. Where did you learn to write like that? – **Very Senior Public Figure**.

- I can guess you can call yourself as one of the good writer now, from what I hear from others – **Grudgingly family member.**

- You know what. Stop this nonsense for working for others. Pay attention on your writings, there is definitely a future for you there – **Work Colleague (Omani).**

- Between Us Only, did you see the new car model? – **Taunting family member on the subject (column).**

- Please send me your last article by E-Mail, I missed it last week – **by many.**

- Do you really have to give us all the time your personal examples? We are tired reading about you – **Omani Senior Engineer**

- One CEO (American) in one establishment had circulated one *article to all his Managers and Head of Departments as 'compulsory' reading, and had even reviewed his own Management style, despite already old on the job !

- I never knew that were Omanis who were such good writers, please keep up the good works to entertain us at least once in the week – **British CEO (anonymous please).**

- You are my best writer – you know me – but will not identify myself for now – because you might not like what you see – but will one day – **Cat Woman.**

- Please send me a copy of your articles before they are printed – **Black Rose.**

- Can I have a copy of your article last week? Missed it, I was in France – **Business Entrepreneur.**

- Can you teach me how to write? – young girl fan.

- Actually I am a great fan of yours! – **Omani Senior Journalist Personality.**

- There is more money for you if you translate your articles in Arabic! – **Omani Journalist and columnist.**

- Mummy, is that the gentleman who writes in the Oman Daily Observer? Ask him! - within earshot – **Young girl (Indian) to her Mum!**

**November 28th 2014**

**Between Us Only! - The Secret!**

**Images - www.istockphoto.com**

**More information and details in my book sites at www.myown-ebooks.com and www.majidbooks.com**

**Also new one at www.myownmajid.com**

**Wipe My Tears!  – www.majidall.com**

# A.08        Doing Good Things To Mankind!

**A      Doing Good Things to Mankind.**

- *The world suffers a lot. Not because of the violence of bad people, But because of the silence of good people! – by Napoleon.*

- **In one of the scenes in The Film – Moses –The Ten Commandments – The Great Prophet (PBUH)** is seen to lament why he was chosen to lead his people and was asking God why it was so - and had not left him alone to be just a simple normal person without this heavy burden and load on his shoulders.

- **In our Islamic Holy Book  - The Holy Quraan - in Surat (verse)  Ad Dhuha – The Glorious Morning Light** – our Great Prophet PBUH is told *3 – Your Guardian Lord Has Not Forsaken You, Nor is He Displeased… 6 – Did He not find you an Orphan and Give you shelter and care?  7 – He found you wandering And he gave you guidance – 8 – And He found you In need, and made you Independent – 9 – Therefore treat not the orphan with harshness 10 – Nor repulse him who asks (needs) – 11- But the Bounty of The Lord Rehearse and Proclaim!*

- **In this Surat (verse),** the vicissitudes of human life are referred to, and a message of hope and consolation is given to man's soul from God's past mercies - and he is bidden to pursue the path of goodness and proclaim the bounties of God.

- One of the people that I greatly admire is Gandhi. On the subject this is what he said – *You must not lose faith in humanity. Humanity is an ocean; if a few drops of the ocean are dirty, the ocean does not become dirty.* He further said – *I look only to the good qualities of men. Not being faultless myself, I won't presume to probe into the faults of others.*

- And then last – but not least – the story of Alexander The Great on his final advice and counsel – that 'he came to the world empty-handed – and in death he is leaving the world – empty handed!

- It is the good things that you do in life that people will remember you by – not your riches, wealth, power and fame.

- Still in writing the book – and not in giving up this being the sixth book – *Writing is the only profession where no one considers you ridiculous if you earn no money* – Jules Renard.

- Writing a book is not an easy task. Besides, there is this comment - ***Writing is the only profession where no one considers you ridiculous if you earn no money – by Jules Renard!***

- As the Author of more than 5 books – and 2 in Arab Management – I should know from my own personal experiences and exposures here! Not to bore you with all the sordid boring details – but you can find all about it in my columns and in my book sites – **www.myown-ebooks.com** – **www.majidbooks.com** and **www.majidalsuleimany.com**

**Between Us Only!  Images – www.istockphoto.com**

# B.00      The Articles

**Images - www.istockphoto.com**

# B.01     **\*\*They Will Not Publish This!**

For a long time now I have been concentrating on propagating my books – **www.myownmajid.com** – rather than commenting on the many articles that have appeared – especially in The English Press – as to Why The Omani Youth Are Not Employable (Into Jobs!). I said I will keep to myself – because for all my life I have been fighting against this theme and focus – and from The First Day I started working in Human Resources after my graduation in 1976! The same slogans – the same emphasis – nothing much has yet changed – despite us not 'escaping The Arab Springs repercussions'!

What made me write this article today is what I saw an 'Expert' British Lady writing in one of The Websites that carried His Majesty Speech to The Omani People! Allah Give him quick recovery, long life and health – Ameen!

In this article this lady had given her opinion why Oman is in Trouble – because Omanisation has failed badly! It is surprising out there that everyone becomes an 'Expert' when it comes to 'why the Omani Youth is NOT EMPLOYABLE in especially The Private Sector!

I do not blame her – because even our Own Columnists say almost the very same things – with bits here and there in variations!

I read also of The Ministry of Information talking the Chief Editors of The Newspapers! Frankly, I think he needed to speak more to The English Press – where 'The Indian Mafia' et al reign supreme under the 'watchful eyes of The Old Guards' – some are not even in that category but more being weak, docile, gullible and naïve lots – rather than having any sort of political touch or bias!

So please forgive me as an ex now retired Human Resources Management Consultant, Professional, Expert and Advisor making my valid pertinent points! Besides, the fact that I published 4 Arab Management Books – (1) Psychology of Arab Management Thinking! – (2) A Cry For Help! – (3) Arab Management: Reality or Myth? The Arab Manager – and (4) The Arab Manager: The Call! – all in my books websites – **www.myownmajid.com** and **www.myown-ebooks.com**

I was also looking at LinkedIn and saw this Indian guy being promoted every time – and this time to Vice President of The Group! And that brings us to the subject matter of today! I have actually worked together with this gentleman! I will say this for him in truth and sincerity! He has the power and knack of bringing in money to the establishment – because he has many workable good ideas!

But if you ask me if I had my own Company – would I employ him? Money coming in or not – the answer is strong negative that I would not! Because he has the worst record of 'negativity' on The Omani Youth – and that stretches even to The Highly Qualified Omanis – because if he had his own way – and he was given Full Authority – NO OMANI WILL BE EMPLOYED BY HIM!

Yet his Sponsors keep promoting him – and look at the other way – because he is bringing in money to the establishment! That is all that mattered here! Nothing less or more!

So please forgive me as I go along here!

I can only relate to things and aspects that I have personally experienced! If The Leadership out there are really interested, they should make someone to READ MY BOOKS – especially The Arab Management ones! They are full of Real True Examples of what is going on! Instead of sending the books as Complimentary Gifts to TOP VIPS – and there is 'not even a slight humanity or decency' of saying thanks for the gift – looking at a gift horse in the mouth! Why? Because deep down in their consciences and hearts – they know I am speaking the TRUTH ONLY!

They should actually translate the books – and make it Compulsory Reading – for everyone from a Director upwards in The Public Sector – and CERTAINLY even in its current forms to all The Top Management in The Companies – especially Those GMs and MDS in Oman over the last 25 years – and NOTHING has really changed on the ground – as far as they are concerned!

But then as we Arabs like to say – There is no one so blind but with eyes but cannot see; no one so deaf but with ears but cannot hear; and no one so dumb but with a mouth but cannot speak! Or as The Romans say – Those that the gods want to destroy – they make them not see, hear or speak!

Besides, the very pertinent and important point – even if I am not that right or correct in my views and assertions – or perhaps right in some but wrong in others etc. – His Majesty has personally allowed his citizens to have an Independent Thinking and Outlooks– as long as they are able to express their views and why they think so!

As a Loyal Citizen, no one can deny me this Right – even if they had 'killed' my columns more on a Technicality rather than anything else!

**Live Example One.**

I wrote about this example before many times! Here was a young Omani Engineering Graduate Lady who was applying in one of the companies I was working as The Head of HR! She had a Degree in Project Management as her Specialisation – and from our own University in SQU. She was applying for a job as a 'Secretary' in one of the jobs that we were advertising! That is the point I want to make here. Usually these things are done by Recruitment – and though I had just taken over from an Indian guy – she too Indian was 'running the show' behind scenes – which I soon put an end to! You as The Omani HR Head MUST BE INTERESTED FIRST!

She was trying to arrange for a Trade Test in Secretary for The Applicants. I told her – I want to see this girl first! Why as an Engineer she is applying for a Secretarial Job? Typical of their lots she cracked jokes that maybe I was interested because she was pretty – or I know the family as she came from Nizwa? Near Manaa – where many Al Suleimanys came from! She was not Al Suleimany anyway!

When she came – I asked her point blank! Are you serious to apply for this job – yet an Engineering graduate? Shame! What she told me shook me to my very foundations – and I can assure you that I am largely built too! She told me – Her Professors had told her it will be easy to get a good Engineering job – even if she was a woman – because of her specialization!

Yet she went to all The Construction and Project Offices companies – and they offered her only Admin, Clerical and Secretarial jobs. All these companies were Indian GMs Managed! One had even the audacity to want her syllabus of the University to see what 'they teach'! These are the same companies that get always LARGE CONSTRUCTION JOBS from the Government – but taking a qualified educated Omani lady was an issue – because they wanted these jobs for their own home lots – unless there were isolated pressures now and then – and mainly from the outside!

I talked to my MD (Nice American Person) and we took her in Inventory Logistics as a Trainee – the nearest thing that was near Engineering! The point I am making here is 'people need to be interested and to get involved' – rather than 'not wanting to rock the boat' – or 'wanting to look nice and good' to especially 'foreigners' – he is our boy! Or girl!

The second incident is nearer home with the same outlooks. My daughter who had an Engineering Degree in Electronics and Electrical – and this time in UK!! Only The MOG companies are 'more serious' than the rest! In some of the Company Websites – the First Question is – Sex? Not the Indian joke one of 3 times a week? But real gender! If you reply Female – an Automatic Reply come up – Sorry! These jobs are only for Male Candidates – even The Project Jobs!

It is so easy to live in a fanciful world. By repeating lies over and over again, in the end people start to believe that 'it is our Education System' that is at fault! I would agree to a certain extent maybe there should be more emphasis on work attitudes, ethics and focuses – but blaming the Education System goes well to 'satisfy the Mafias – mainly Indian led – with due apologies here – and certainly The Old Guards who want NO CHANGES – or Rocking The Boat!

I would recommend moving all those Expatriates in Top Positions who have been there for the last 20 years plus and bring in New Blood – if there are no Omani takers! But certainly MORE RISK TAKING of putting Omani 'that care and feel for their own' – and are also similarly inclined For More Risk Taking of their subordinate Omanis – and VALUE AND ESTEEM their own more – rather than putting candidates of 'Our own Boys' and Girls' who will do our bidding – or do as we tell them to do!

Also it is High Time to stop all these advertisements in especially English Newspapers of Visitors looking for a job – and a Special Division be created that sends such Applicants back home for such visits under 'guise of Tourism' when actually they are coming here for jobs – and silly games being played to deny our own jobs because of such temporary filling of jobs by these lots!

I know I am burning my bridges behind me – and building more enemies at the same time! But no one can do these things except ourselves only!

Please REMEMBER His Majesty is sick person – and we should not trouble him by these things that we can do ourselves as a start!

**With sincere genuine apologies!**

**Majid Al Suleimany**
**The Author**

**November 28, 2014**

**\*\* Especially The Oman English Press and Media!**

## B.02        My Last Oman Observer Articles!

**From The Coast!**

http://majidwrite.com/2013/07/23/from-the-coast-oman-tv-presentation/

**Read it as above!**

**Everything good has to come to an end one day! ALR.**

**All my articles including the above – are incorporated in my new Book – Wipe My Tears!**

**Wishing All My Readers and Fans All The Best.**

**And apologies to any of my adversaries – and those who did not like me – and my articles!**

**Goodbye – And Maa Salamah!**

**Best wishes and regards,**

**Majid Al Suleimany**

**From One of My Strongest Fan! Indian -**

As you mentioned in one of your previous mails after some time one would give up. How long one would swim against the tide, either swim with them or die trying for a change. LOL

Just sharing what is in my heart, this is my personal view…

## B.03        Solving Our Own Problems!

### Thursday – July 11th 2013.

- *O, mankind, we have created you from a male and a female; and We have made you into tribes and sub-tribes that you may recognise one another. Verily, the most honourable among you, in the sight of Allah, is he who is most righteous among you. Surely Allah is All-Knowing, All-Aware –* **The Holy Quran – Ch.49: V.14**

- *O ye who believe! Be steadfast in the cause of Allah, bearing witness in equity: and let not a people's enmity incite you to act otherwise than with justice. Be always just, that is nearer to righteousness. And fear Allah, Surely Allah is aware of what you do –* **The Holy Quran – Ch.5: V.9**

- *The Believers are but a single Brotherhood: so make peace and reconciliation between your two (contending) brothers; and fear Allah that you may receive Mercy –* **Holy Quran – 49:10**

**Before I write on today's topic** – it is the Holy Month of Ramadhan. It is the month for deep soul searching ourselves and in self-analysis – and in trying to rectify and to amend our ways and methods to the right ways and path – Amin. It is also the month for forgiveness and in reconciliation. It is also the month of 'talking to one another' – and saying what is in our hearts!

Having said that, it needs to be pointed out that as a Writer and Columnist – I hate writing about topics that are sensitive like religion and politics – because as a person I believe in live and let live syndrome – and that everyone has a right for living as best as one can under the true basic humanity rights – and our true values and focuses in the society – without hindrance and interference from any other!

Also though I try my best to follow my religion and its teachings and principles – I am not an expert or learned in such affairs – nor will I ever try to profess as such ever in my life – so please forgive me! Nor am I a Political or Military Analyst for that matter! I am also not pro or against Morsi – as is not my concern. Those who have read my book Psychology of Arab Management Thinking will also note on this and why! Also I am not Egyptian – it is only for them to decide – whom they want as President – or not!

**Images – Demonstrations!**

It was just by coincidence that I had watched the carnage destructive attack by the Egyptian forces on supposed to be unarmed civilians supposed to be peaceful demonstrators that wanted their elected president reinstated! It is not my intention to get brawled into all the aspects of what really happened – the truths, not the truths – and the fabricated – as it is not my business in reality! Bottom line several innocent lives were lost – including those of children – and babies too! And this as people were supposed to be praying Fajr prayers too!

I watch with great sadness and heavy heart of a great country like Syria being destroyed at the helm – a full blown out civil war and destruction – and not only by their own people – but also from outsiders – supporting one side from the other! From what started as a simple graffiti incident of 25 students – how it was bungled up and mishandled – to current status quo – of a great country going into utter ruins, destruction, malaise and decadence! I ask myself the fundamental question – Who really has benefited – and still stands to benefit?

**Images - Demonstrations!**

**I look at these below – and wonder – do we really know of all these things in reality?**

- *Abu Bakrah (R.A.) narrated "I heard Allah's Messenger (SAW) saying, When two Muslims fight (meet) each other with their swords, both the murderer as well as the murdered will go to Hell-fire." I said, "O Allah's Messenger! It is all right for the murderer but what about the murdered one? Allah's Messenger replied, "He surely had the intention to kill his companion –* **Bukhari, Vol. 1, Hadith 30**

- *O ye who believe! If a wicked person comes to you with any news, ascertain the truth, lest ye harm people unwittingly, and afterwards become full of repentance for what ye have done –* **Qur'an 49:6**

- *O ye who believe! Take not the Jews and the Christians for your friends and protectors; They are but friends and protectors to each other; And he amongst you that turns to them is one of them. Surely, Allah Guides not a people unjust –* **Quran 5:51**

**I wonder out aloud** – human beings never cease to surprise and amaze at what they are really capable of – and doing to others – and as if nothing will ever happen to them – because they are fully covered – and have all the protection they need! But are we really sure? Have we read and analysed the situation correctly? Have we compared notes to what happened to others – and elsewhere before all these things?

There is a famous East African saying that says when brothers fight – take your plough and go to farm – that is metaphorically 'Do not get involved!' – Because when they patch up – you will end as the loser! There is also the Arabic saying that if my brother fights my brother – I will try to bring them together – and not get involved. But if my brother fights my cousin – I will support my brother. But if my cousin fights someone else – I will support my cousin!

It is high time for us all to wake up from this deep self-induced slumber – and wake up to the truth and realities – and facts of life – before it is too late for all of us! Amin.

- *Help one another in righteousness and piety, but help not one another in sin and rancor: Fear Allah for Allah's strict in punishment* – **The Holy Quran 5:2**

- *We cannot solve our problems with the same level of thinking that created them* – **Albert Einstein**

- *The best way to resolve any problem in the human world is for all sides to sit down and talk* – **Dalai Lama**

- *The difference between what we do and what we are capable of doing would suffice to solve most of the world's problems* – **Mahatma Gandhi**

- *The whole problem with the world is that fools and fanatics are always so certain of themselves, and wiser people so full of doubts* – **Bertrand Russell**

Yesterday one of my very good friends ST  had died after being very sick for a very long time – so please forgive me for being so emotional and sensitised – because none of us know what is waiting for us all ahead in life! Before we meet our Maker – and end in eternal damnation and hell fire – and from the moment we are lowered down into our graves!

May Allah God direct us to the right ways and path – Amin. Ramadhan Kareem Greetings! Take Care!

By Majid Al Suleimany

## B.04        The Role of Advisors!

**For Sunday – July 7th 2013.**

- **Be very careful in what you are wishing for!**
- **You may get your wish to come true!**
- **Be careful in choosing your Advisors – they can make – or break you!**
- **Do you remember the fable of The Emperor's New Clothes?**

Human beings never cease to surprise and amaze at what they are really capable of – and doing to others – and as if nothing will ever happen to them – because they are fully covered – and have all the protection they need! But are we really sure? Have we read and analysed the situation correctly? Have we compared notes to what happened to others – and elsewhere before all these things?

There is a famous East African saying that when brothers fight – take your plough and go to farm – that is metaphorically 'Do not get involved!' – Because when they patch up – you will end as the loser!

There is also the Arabic saying that if my brother fights my brother – I will try to bring them together – and not get involved. But if my brother fights my cousin – I will support my brother. But if my cousin fights someone else – I will support my cousin!

**Images – Advisors!**

It is also being said that in one ex colonial ruled country, the Dictator was asking his Team of Advisors – that he wanted to reverse the traffic system of the country from what it was now of people driving on the left to driving opposite to the right. He formed a panel compromising several engineers, experts and intellectuals to come up with a concrete and feasible plan on how to do the change. He was driven by bringing change to the ways of the colonial masters.

After several months and follow-ups the Advisors came up to the conclusion that the plan was not feasible due to very high costs in transformation and changes to the traffic layout and infrastructure – and it was a nightmare plan to even think off – let alone to implement! But everybody was scared to tell the bad news to the Dictator – for fear of real heads to roll if one tried to do this!

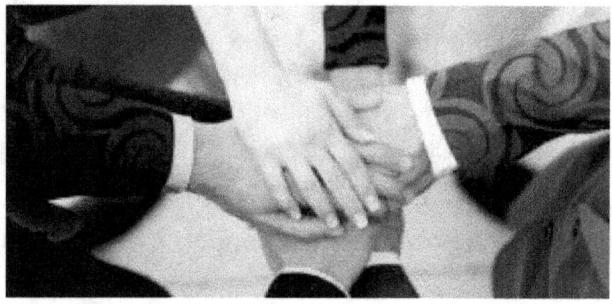

**Images - Advisors!**

So they drew lots of who would tell the Dictator. It finally dawned on one Engineer who was distantly related to the Dictator – as a possible way out of the impasse situation. He tried his best to convey the message to the Dictator. Luckily for him the man was in a good mood that day – and he did nothing untoward the messenger of bad news! Then he took the advisor aside and told him – try to see if we can at least have the big trucks go on the right for now – whilst the rest go on the left. Maybe this can work! The Engineer Advisor was baffled – because this was a sure way of increasing that fast the rate of accidents and fatalities in the country!

There are several cases reported later in history where very bad decisions were made but the Advisors were all impotent and helpless – and in fear and dread – to advise correctly and ethically because they feared for their lives' if they said the truth to the especially draconian autocratic dictators!

Forgive me for those that really know of the advisor joke and if I had missed out the punch line! There are many other such advisors' jokes – you can Google them! I liked also about the one of the last advisor who gave the advice to the Dictator of how he could make the whole country happy – though it is usually one group of people making the very same joke about the other group of people always!

During my career life, I have been fooled and hoodwinked that the top brass were really interested in getting ideas, feedback and research on the aspects, issues and tasks at hand! It was more a front and façade to show 'things were changing and improving' – and not really find out the real core and real truth of things and the situation per se!

**Images - Advisors!**

I have a very clever family member who always would try to figure out what the boss really wanted – and would make him very happy by giving the same advice back to him. His outlook was – why should I be bothered – if I can get all I want from the situation – and I have lost nothing from the equation? The boss is happy – and I am happy too!

**Images – Advisors!**

We both gain from the situation – and if anything would go wrong in the plan – or its execution – he would always reiterate that he had given the boss a choice of options – and it is the boss that had opted for this one! Remember boss? The boss cannot deny it – because they usually only remember his own preferred option – and he had conveniently forgotten the other options – or even if they had been made in the first instance!

Then when things have turned out wrong and sour – the boss has only himself to blame – because of listening to his own advices – but coming out from another person's mouth – which is all in reality that he had wanted in the first place – but was using all kinds of cover and disguise to get at it!

**Image – Advisor!**

I said this in my column years back! As kids we used to be that much scared of our father – that even one day he was reversing the truck into a coconut tree – and we dared not to shout at him to stop! Even though we were all sitting at the back of the truck – and we were most likely to be hurt in the process! Our late father got out from the truck – took a look at the slightly dented American Ford truck – and for the first time he saw the funny and the humourous part of his own dictatorial and autocratic ways – a joke he kept telling his friends for a long time after! The only thing he asked was – Why did you not tell me?  To complete silence and no answer even!

**Image – Advisor!**

In one of the most ugly and vulgar experiences as a Human Resources Consultant and Advisor – we were given names of some staff that we should come forward to 'volunteer to the company' as people marked out for release and termination – and a few others for fast development and progression! This came out after we had said we had interviewed most of the Staff – and what were their training and other requirements! Of course, we refused to participate in the sham scam business – and not only were we denied further business – but the payment for the current job was considerably delayed.

In one other incident at another place, we were even asked to give full names 'of who said what, where and when' – when we were conducting a Staff Morale (Climate) Survey! The more disturbing part was not that this was asked of us in the first instance – but that as they said – 'others had consented to this request before' – and we reiterated we were not like them! That too ended with the business side – with me resisting the urge from others high up 'to please participate and join with them' in this!

In one person I sent my books to, he gave the books to his Advisor – If you want them – that is parting remark! Please keep remembering all these things happened years ago – and I do not know if things have now really changed on the grounds – but I sincerely hope it has!

**Take Care!**

**By Majid Al Suleimany**

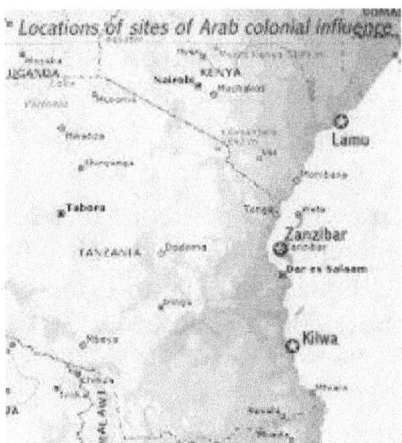

**Image – From The Coast!**

## B.05        From The Coast!

**Oman Television Presentation!**

**For Thursday – July 25th 2013.**

**Between Us Only!**

**http://omanobserver.om/node/170271**

*From The Coast* is a new Oman TV production series of 30 episodes about Oman and Zanzibar – and is being shown during the Holy month of Ramadhan 2013. Every day after Iftar Breakfast at 19.30hrs. You can find Episode 1 and links to the rest here

https://www.youtube.com/watch?v=p1oOXtP2xLU&feature=youtube_gdata_player

The series carry many highly personalized emotional and sensitive topics to many of us all pertaining to the relationships – but particularly to the remaining in the islands of original Omani descent and ancestry! In one case there is an interview with HE The Minister of Foreign Affairs Yousuf Alawi – and his personal take and views on the subject – which was a great eye opener for even me thought well versed with the topic!

The programme refreshes our memories about these bygone glorious days. It is noteworthy that the 25 minute programme directed by Ahmed al Hadri will be shown during the whole of Ramadhan. The director is delighted that he has been able direct a cultural programme that would bring back a beautiful and magnificent life spent in Zanzibar.

There are many other sensitive, dramatic and highly emotional topics – for example in one of the interviwees – who looks all Omani in every aspect – refusing to talk to the TV Crew because 'he is still angry that he has not been successful to return to Oman' – though some of his children did! That brings us to the discussion point that there are many families here like him who have families split between those still there – and some who did return. In my own family – I have had uncles and aunts there – with the families there still – and though some of them do still wish to come – with the majority that did come back in the early 1970s – they are not able to!

**Images – Zanzibar!**

**Images – Zanzibar & Coast!**

I believe an Indian crew – and others too for that matter – could also run a similar programme of now as Omanis – but there originality coming from India and the other places too. In one of my returning trips to Oman from a course in UK – there was this British man in front of me for the queue for only Omanis and The GCC. So M being M – without closing his mouth – and removing all doubt! Politely pointed out to him that he was in the wrong queue! To which the good man turned to me waving his Omani passport – and curtly remarking – *You mean this will not work here?* He cleared faster than I was able to – anyway! And that told me a lot of things – some perhaps I may not have preferred to have heard then!

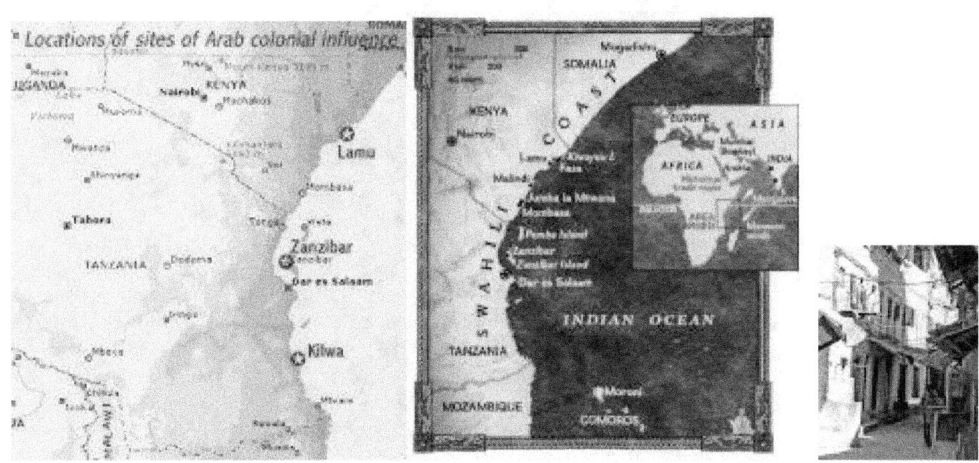

**Images – Zanzibar & Coast!**

We too have family members that are citizens of other countries all over the world – USA, UK, Canada, India etc – and apart of those that the programme is supposed to cover – from Somalia all the way down to Mozambique even – and to the West of

Africa to Ruanda, Burundi, Zaire and The Congos! Part and parcel of the only non-European colonial empire that belonged to Oman then! In some of the places – though under different flags and nationalities – even for the locals – they hold dear close fond memories of their times under The Oman Empire then! A great nation and reckoning power that was able to put its name, records and history – legacy, destiny etc. with colonial nations like British, France and others.

Researchers and social scientists – and in our future Omani youngsters especially – need to make a study of what had happened that this great power went that down that fast – if we even were there before the so-called great colonialists came well after us even – in many cases – and even in history records the colonialists had to come to Oman allegiances to 'solve many of their problems that they were facing at the time – and Omani allegiances came to save the day for them – and everyone else around them for that matter! Perhaps even we had put too much trust and confidence with others that we thought were our friends – and had our best interests at heart – whilst quietly underground working against us – in harmful destructive wanton ways – whilst we lived in delusion and in wishful thinking!

Images – Zanzibar & Coast!

And the same thing being repeated all over again – then and in the later chapters of history – and whilst we continue to have the self-induced slumber – because and whilst we look at the smaller things in life – and cannot see the bush because of the trees – the bigger picture – and looking outside the box even! The truth cannot be denied that even great and powerful nations like USA, UK and France – have many minority ethnic citizens that had originated from the other countries – and especially from their ex colonies like UK and France cases – and the later constituting to even more than 10% of the total population even!

I was watching this highly emotional programme of under 18 youth in Norway coming together to protect a young girl of 16 – who was inadvertently a Muslim! It made me feel so bad 'with quick decisions of choosing sides' that I got it all wrong at the programme start – and as a human being with feelings and care for others – and human beings coming to do the right, correct and ethical thing – even if late and inadvertently – had made me feel that guilty – that I could not stop the tears even!

Sometimes I just cannot stop admiring the 'adversary' – because for countries like in Israel – whether you are black, brown or white – you are a Jew first – and if even they will kick out the 'original owners of the land' – to make space for their own people wherever they came from different parts of the world – even from Ethiopia! I read in The Hadith of Allah God of those people that help and support one another – and wonder out aloud maybe that could be the reason that they are always winning and victorious?

One cannot just stop thinking along these lines, anyway! Oman TV should make the programmes translated into English, French, German etc. so that a wider audience of the world can get a hold of its great powerful message – of a great powerful Arab Nation – that had not only made and created history in the world – but a force to be reckoned – recognised and to be admired too!

Thanks to Oman TV – and MOI. I have carried a lot of the East African stories in my books – especially The Between Us Only! Series – more information here and at **www.myownmajid.com** – some serious – but many funny anecdotes – and certainly worth reading – and not time-waters! But do not just take my word for it!

Happy 43$^{rd}$ Renaissance Day – May Allah Give HM long life and health – Amin, And for my British fans – great news, indeed, for the new third in line to the throne baby boy – and my guess is he is going to be called Michael?

**Images – Zanzibar & Coast – For Demonstration Purposes Only!**

**Ramadhan  Mubarak –  Please do remember your 'poorer relatives' here and abroad! Take Care!**

**By Majid Al Suleimany**

**THE FINAL OBSERVER ARTICLE....!!**

## B.06        My Most Vivid Dream!

### The Sequel!

**In one of my articles**, that I had written as a young boy for a National Writing Competition in that distant land was titled – *My Most Vivid Dream!* I have never given so much details until now what I had really dreamt in that dream – because sometimes it is better that way! But in a nutshell the dream had never turned to reality – but only to find myself instead – with my family – returning to Oman – after my late father had left for East Africa as a young man with 2 of his children – my late elder brother and sister aged then at 12 and 10 respectively!

As Muslims, we believe that once someone has died – there is no sort of communication between the dead and living! I was talking to one famous Religious Scholar one day and telling him about a dream I had of my late father coming to me to console me – and this was at a time when I was very sad and distraught about the things that were facing me in my life then!

**Images – Dreams!**

My late Father had put me on a coconut tree and he was shaking the tree like a child's swing! All the time trying to console and comfort me! The Religious Scholar was visibly upset that I believed in such things – and was trying to convince me 'that it was a big sin' to believe in such things! In the end, seeing I was not agreeing with him – and wanting to depart on cool terms he added that 'because we think too much on these things – that is why such dreams come to us!

Anyway, last night a bit disappointed – because I thought today Thursday August 8th would be Eid – being a diabetic case and finding it more hard and difficult as the years go by – I had another of these mirage dreams!

**Images – Dreams!**

It all comes from all these continuous disappointments I had with the said Newspaper and also some delicate intricate family issues – and perhaps the reason why I had dreamt again! This time my late Father was a bit angry and disappointed with me! He was saying to me 'to stop hurting yourself and banging your head against brick walls – making it swollen and red – and that you are just wasting your time, efforts and energies – because you cannot 'change anything in the society' – like I had told you before many times – but you still you do not listen to me!

**Please stop these things now – he implored – and almost begged me – before I woke up with a start!**

**Eid Greetings!**

**By Majid Al Suleimany**

**August 8, 2013**

## B.07      Things Have Simply Not Really Changed!

- *To send a letter is a good way to go somewhere without moving anything but your heart* - **Phyllis Theroux**

**Today I tried my best** – and avoided to get embroiled into an argument with one – sorry to say it to those of my friends! – An Indian Top Sales Marketing guy – a Services Provider that I have been using for a number of years. Have given them good business in the past – and the relationships are to mutual advantages, anyway!

There is no point to continue banging my head against brick walls – and just making it swollen and red in the process!

Five years ago, I had formally reported this same guy to his Indian Superiors – and I went so far to report him formally to The Company Owners – who though are Omanis – but are also of Indian descent.

The person promised to change and behave – but simply has not! In treating even qualified, experienced and professional Omanis with complete disdain and contempt. The mind just boggles of how he treats the Junior Younger Omanis under him.

I have stopped writing now my columns in The Oman Daily Observer – because there too things have not changed that much to date?

I have written two books in Management in these issues – **http://www.myownmajid.com** – and several column articles before – so what is the use, anyway I do not know how long these things will continue – before there is a breaking point?

The problems with us Omanis are that we are very welcoming, respecting and esteeming to 'The Invited Guests' in our country – unalike even others near us! Thus the few of them especially feel it is okay to 'shit over our heads' in forgetting the famous expression – Biting the hand that feeds you …and ending as proved in many cases – of 'licking the boot that kicks you'!!

I am not a Political Scientist or Expert – but since yesterday Wednesday I have never ever felt so sad in my life ever before – because all the things I have said and cautioned about have come to pass – and I feel so sad, unhappy and miserable to keep saying – I have said it, before! Or I told you so!

Even at the dangers of losing something so nice and good that you had never had before or expected – and something you should strive to protect, defend and let it grow and prosper – the evilness and selfishness in people will just not change – even if they know their actions – or inactions – would lead to what, where and when!

**May Allah God Protect and Preserve us all – from His Anger and Fury – Amin.**

**So Sad.**

**Majid al Suleimany**

**Thursday – August 15th 2013.**

**Things Have Really Not Changed**

## B.08        Do Not Cry For Me!

**Further my below -**

http://majidwrite.com/2013/08/15/things-have-really-not-changed/

**From a good American Friend -**

Maybe you should consider our place here. Here we do respect The Elders – especially The Learned Ones like you. Sad you have a Great Religion – but you do not simply follow it! I feel desolate to see the carnages in Egypt.

**From an Omani Enthusiast**

I think it is time to let go the Indians especially – and particularly those that have been with so for so long! They are the worser kinds than the newer ones, although they too get influenced easily by the same lots! Anyway, our younger ones are getting smarter – and they will solve all these problems for us and even sooner than we are thinking of! Mark my words!

http://www.hurriyetdailynews.com/egypt-shame-for-islam-arab-world-turkish-president-gul-says.aspx?pageID=238&nID=52700&NewsCatID=338

دموع اردوغان في صلاة الغائب على شهداء مصر في تركيا
لا تبكى ايها القائد العظيم وربى القصة الصبر قادم ان شاء الله

**What more can I say now?**

- *The only reason for being a professional writer is that you can't help it!*

    Leo Rosten

**B.09        Points To Ponder!**

August 13, 2013

**A            Young Marriages in Troubles!**

 I was inquiring about one young couple with young children – that we know well – why they had not come to visit us this Eid – as they usually do! I was told – Have you not heard? Heard what? – I asked back!

Then they told me that this beautiful couple had divorced a few backs. It seems the main issues were mainly money related – each one building his and her own villa. The problems that there was so much concentration on 'building a decent large villa' that family living expenses and expenditures took a direct hit!

I read somewhere that internationally one of the major reasons of divorces was 'money related'. It is very sad because these young children will be most affected by this divorce – because the innocent children will not understand and appreciate what has just happened – and how was it possible that the people that loved them this so much – hated each other so vehemently and disastrously – to go their different ways – just for money! Like I have said so many times before – it is the children that get most hit and affected in such cases!

We have still not learnt our lessons – despite all of our Religious Teachings, The Holy Book and The Islamic Hadith – that our lives on this earth are just a temporary phase – and a transition to a Greater World! It reminded me also of reading about The Great King Alexander Story – 'I came to the world empty-handed – and I leave to my grave empty-handed! I go with my hands out in my coffin – and as I leave behind all my treasures and wealth – and cannot take it with me even!'

## B          Ants versus Us Humans!

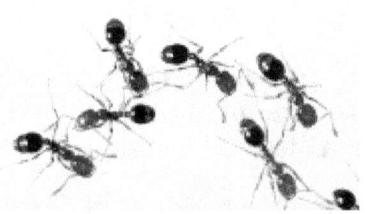

I was watching these ants in my villa garden in Qorum Heights- and as I was eating this chicken sandwich! A small piece of chicken had fallen on the floor – and who comes along at top speed but this small black ant! I watch intrigued as the ant starts pulling the piece towards what I expect to be its ant hill entrance! I was really intrigued in its unselfishness – and its determination to pull this 'morsel' to share with others – and even if it was almost three times its own size!

I was thinking aloud that if this was 'a human being' – it would first make sure it had a full feed of the morsel – or even keeping it for himself only! Yet here it was determined to give its full strength and abilities to share with others! As far as I could tell – it had not even taken a bite of the 'morsel' for itself – but had instead willed and determined to share – first and foremost – with others first!

Ants can teach us humans a lot of things. I respected this ant so much – and I just left it alone! I could not bring myself to harm it in anyway – even if I had tried! Soon other ants came to help the ant! I decided to leave then – because knowing us human beings – I would find the entrance – and kill and destroy all the ants!

This is a great achievement for the ants – when even your worst enemy has just but to admire you – and leave you alone to your fate – be it whatever it is!

**Take Care!**

**By**

**Majid Al Suleimany**

**August 13, 2013**

**N.B. I would appreciate responses here or to majidsn@majidsuleimany.com if it is worth continuing posting these kind of articles here in view of ending of my Oman Daily Observer Columns?**

**Alternatively, maybe just closing down the sites?**

**Regards,**

**Majid Al Suleimany - August 14th 2013**

## B.10        In All Seriousness ….!

## http://main.omanobserver.om/node/137207

**I am going to say this a last time – and then we will continue with lesser topics as lately!**

Some people may think that I may be naïve and stupid - but I can assure you that I am fully aware that despite the given facts that I am a fully qualified and experienced Omani National Human Resources professional, expert and advisor – I do not receive even temporary consultancy jobs now – because people are simply afraid on what I might write – especially on those companies!

In all seriousness – last two weeks back I got this message from a good Indian friend of mine who was promoted and though now heading a small section – he was now going to report now directly to the CEO – an Omani! The guy has been in Oman over 30 years now – and like Johnny Walker – is still going strong! Then I learnt of another expatriate case where the person has now even retired in Oman in his job – though he came to Oman at the age of 25! He also reports to an Omani CEO.

**Image - An Omani Engineer**

Let us put our cards on the table! I am not denying the facts that these two people were very committed, dedicated, good and talented in their jobs – that is why they were kept on! As a HR professional – it would be not doing my job – if I do not admit this.

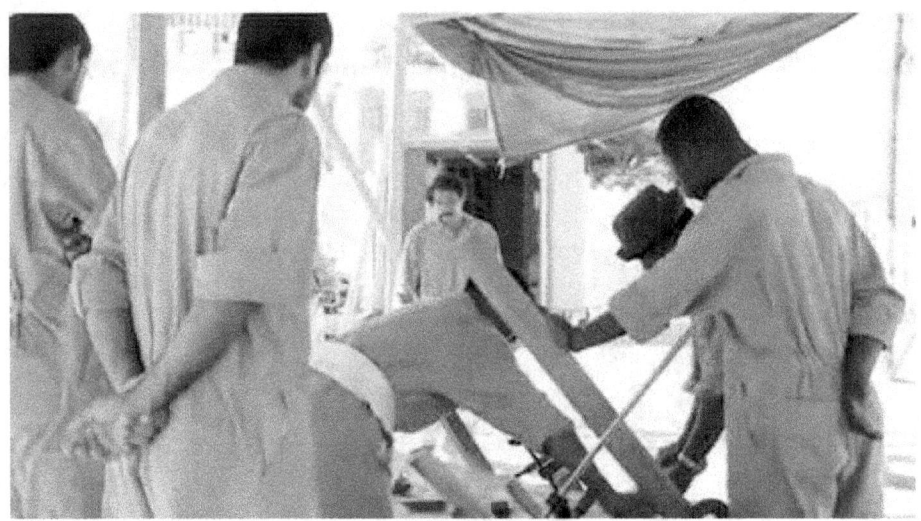

**Image - Learning on the job!**

We had another example of a 'friend CEO' - Omani too - who gave away my job to an Indian guy – because he 'was cheaper – and part of his outlooks – in being able to easier control and dominate people below him – and not the money factor alone. Despite the fact that he was heading a 'national company' that was dedicated to offer jobs to experienced and qualified Omanis first and paramount! My disqualification came in 'being obstinate and not towing the line – the 'drop dead and lie still' syndrome.

In another example, a 'friend Omani CEO' wanted to recruit a woman engineer from one country 'because she looked so pretty – and nice to have around in the offices' – as he smugly put it – tongue in cheek! Despite me also cautioning him – as my job required me to do so – that her both written and spoken English were below the required levels. Though calling himself as a religious pious person – he certainly would not extend the same treatment to an Omani lady engineer – however pretty she looked!

**Image - All The Omani Air Hostesses!**

**Future Omani Lady Engineers**

The common formulae in all these is the same – if local CEOs could do these to their own lots – why do we want and expect expatriate CEOs and GMs to be different? People see these things going on live – and they copy and emulate! If people cannot be kind and compassionate to one another – and we bring in dirty polarisation and politicking in – what else can be the results?

They also say charity begins at home! If we are so hard and uncompromising on our own – how can the good Lord Protect and Preserve us from harm and dangers of all kinds and sorts – because the concept of 'neighbours' is paramount in our religion – because of the concept of brotherhood and being one in the faith and in the beliefs!

At one time if you went to the Banks - you could hardly find any Omanis – maybe a few clerks at junior levels – a driver – PRO – gardener – tea boy etc. There were hardly any Branch Managers – Managers - senior officers – except isolated very few! These now have risen to be in Management – and even GMs and CEOs. today! There are still some expatriates in head offices more – but in the branches they are almost all Omanised! Perhaps a peg or two in services went down – but if you consider the volume of traffic of customers and all the lots – overall they are doing very good competent professional services – and are all dedicated and committed overall!

The same thing can be said of the oil companies – from the time I joined in 1970s where even the toilets and dining rooms were segregated – by seniority – and the seniors were mainly expatriates – with few isolated cases of Omanis coming in at lower levels as clerks and technicians!

I am not bragging – but in my Arab Management books – I said almost the very same things and aspects – covering over 35 years in my career life and with live personal experiences and exposures!

Apart from a few bad apples and eggs – each basket has some – given the right opportunities, breaks and chances – coupled with the right ethical, principled and professional approaches, guidance, mentorship and counselling – Omanis youngsters especially have risen to the occasion – and overall not that disappointing and letting down syndromes – as others would like them to be – and that includes our own – and the 'old guards' not excluded!

We are all talking about Omanis preferring to work in the public sector. I have not seen yet a study as to why this is so – but all kinds of theories and concepts – many not yet proven! But the truth can be this – in my offering to volunteer some ideas – if even senior qualified Omanis cannot survive in some places – how can the youngsters?

Especially if the theme and focus is 'to control and dominate' – and any raised voices are to be subdued. I have said this in my article – The Offices Mini Dictators – and that includes 'fellow local friends CEOs and GMs too – and even The Board in some places!

May the Good Lord Protect and Preserve us all – Amin – but changes and focuses are still required - where in some places you still have to look around for Omanis! And those that come in simply cannot survive and exist – because of the hidden agendas and manifestos – the Mafia gangs – and admittedly though from a few quarters – are still in control and in dominating! Including our own too for that matter!

**Bottom Line – Change has indeed come! Change now – before change changes you! Take Care!**

By Majid Al Suleimany

Posted at: www.majidall.com and at www.majidwrite.com

## B.11        The Jobs Applicants!

### For Thursday - June 27th 2013.

- *Our young men have proven over the past years that they are people of resolve* - **Abdicating Emir of Qatar in favour of his son speech June 25th 2013.**

- *Every day I wake up a little afraid. Only a fool is never afraid!* – **Ron Meyer**

- *If you do not tell the truth about yourself; you cannot tell it about other people!* – **Virginia Woolf**

I read now with great interests about The Jobs Applicants – and how that from the so-called for interviews lots – that many do not turn up even – or if the minority do – they turn down the offers as too little! And not to their expectations!

I do not know what has really happened or changed – but a few years ago the situation was not that rosy! Whatever jobs that were offered – people 'ran to grab' – the only issues remained of high demands and expectations – and of people moving around jobs – and changing for even as little as Omani Rials 30 in the 'live examples' per se that I had handled myself – and in trying to talk to them and to convince them 'not to leave' – because we had a career plan for them – and were looking at their best interests – even if it may take a bit longer!

But the wait was better – for their overall interests and benefits! Some of them listened – but many did not! Years far later in life I see them in the very same jobs and levels – whilst their peers that were more attentive to good advices and wisdoms – have moved on – to higher levels! To levels that even for some of them were pleasantly surprising – and least expected!

I know personally of many cases that some that are now Senior Managers and Directors – but their 'rolling stone gathers no moss' peers are at best at middle levels – and that too if they are lucky! That happens to you when you leave a good decent place – for another with a few more Rials – and who are more interested in poaching others trained – to 'boost their egos and Omanisation figures only – and not really interested in the person in reality – or what he represents.

Generally this happens in mainly expatriate management run companies – and everyone knows this! Does not even need to be said – but as the good Brits say – 'that is how the cookie crumbles! Despite so many things happening – nothing much has happened in these places in reality – with exception of the new media gimmicks of 'office parties and long services recognition awards – but apart from that nothing concrete or in reality! The PRO and the Clerk is still there – same levels – years on – years out – whilst his peer is a Supervisor, Asst. Manager – or even a Manager – in the place he left and quickly abandoned for 30 Omani Rials more! It is very sad and pathetic in reality!

There is an expression that says – Do not kill the messenger. Over 10 years ago – in my first book I wrote about 'The Rebellious Teenagers' – giving live examples – but as usual people do not like these to hear these things – and want to be fooled by always hearing only good news – not the other lot! It is still there – and people can still read it!

In one acrimonious Management meeting – even before this – can you imagine? I had cautioned about the problems of jobs – and the flimsy excuses we were giving at the time of turning away job aspirants – and yet people will always compare 'apples to oranges' – when they see many other expatriates – and in large numbers – still working there! If I were in a place where people read my columns – and act on my advices – I firmly believe we could have avoided a lot of things. Yet in this meeting I was clearly sidelined and marginalised – and for a long time after that! For the first time that year I received 'Just Satisfactory' performance bonus – when in many years before it was in the superior levels – as a personal message and affront!

I find it very satirical that the same peoples that are now retired too – telling me that they 'heard me loud and clear' – and really appreciated my personal sacrifices vis-à-vis my career progression and prospects! But the part that makes me find it more jovial and pun – is saying 'we were just following orders – do not blame us'! I guess even the Nazis cold tell the same to the 6 million massacred Jews in the holocaust – if they wanted to! Or in Rwanda – and so many other examples!

Going back to the Job Applicants. In one of the places I was working there was an Omani girl Engineering graduate and SQU too – who had applied for a Secretarial job that we had advertised to replace the expatriates – as 'jobs reserved for Omanis' – at least at those times! I asked her point blank if she was crazy or what? She told me – I come from the Interior – I know no one with W here – and even our own do not help us! And I am the only bread winner now – with my sick parents resisting the urge to marry me off to a richer man with 2 wives already – till I finished my studies!

When the good American CEO came on a visit from Dubai – I told him this heart rending story of this young Omani girl! The good man told me – You are the Country HR Manager – and make a proposal so we both can recruit her in the Secretarial Slot – but we will move her to look after Logistics and Inventory – which is the 'nearest Engineering' job that we had at the time! It was done – and she was recruited.

Yet this same girl had gone to many local Engineering Companies – run by expatriate Management. And they told her the very same thing – we do not have any Engineering jobs now – but we can take you in Admin. Admin being the dumping grounds for University graduates – and these same firms are everyday now in the days in various campaigns – and winning all kinds of 'home country awards' – and for what? For deceiving and hoodwinking peoples – because like in this case they would have had to train and educate her – and there were no 'good American CEO and caring local HR Manager' around! Forgive me – for blowing my own trumpet!

**What more can I say now? Take Care!**

**By Majid Al Suleimany**

# B.12        A Question of Payments!

**For Sunday - June 30<sup>th</sup> 2013.**

- *I propose that we abandon our relations entirely. I shall lose nothing by it, for my own emotional tie with you has long been a thin thread - the lingering effects of past disappointments* - **Letter from Dr. Freud to Discipline Jung in association relationships breakup in 1913.**

**I have been watching now with increasing alarm, tensions, aggravations** and apprehensions concerning the situation vis-à-vis due payments to people – customers, clients and others – and sadly from even well-established supposed to be high profile places – and to the extent that the situation just stinks of just malaise, decadence and decay only! It is so pathetic, disheartening and disappointing that words can no longer describe the situation anymore – and has gone over board for any retraction or retribution.

A long time ago when the rumours were spreading that our Consultancy was closing down – we saw the true picture of people and what they really were 'when the issue of money' came in – and they showed us their true colours and mantle that they were hiding so long as the situation was rosy and good – and business was still going their way!

You may not believe this but in a way with the Arab expression 'that from evil came great tidings' – or as the Brits say – 'the rainbow after the rains' – to come into absolute shock and dismay of how nasty and ugly people can turn when money issues come in! There are no borders – and all the red lines are crossed – quite easily too!

In one of the situations that the East Africans call carving your face – kuchonga uso – a good friend of mine took me to one VIP business man with a lot of companies under him! He is surrounded by Expatriate Managers in his family business – and one who frequently even visits the home for dinner uninvited! We were at his one day – me and my Indian lady Assistant with even a previously arranged appointment to meet in his house!

We were put in the waiting room – and asked politely if we wanted any soft drinks, tea or coffee? My Indian Assistant as usual just asked for a glass of water – which she hardly drank – but that is a different story for now. The parting remark of the attendant was 'boss and family' were having dinner – and with my usual put my foot in my mouth style started joking 'why boss did not invite us for dinner – especially as he knew we were coming? The poor attendant fidgeted quite intensively – not used to such cracks – and what to answer instead! Anyway, this great expatriate Assistant came out with him – after the dinner – and hopefully there were vegetarian food there too – or the person was not observing anymore!

The person from the beginning was against 'helping us out' – though he had admitted years later that he could – if he really had wanted! I reiterated to him that it was God's mysterious ways of working – because that is how I had ended and moved to writing – and becoming an Author of 8 books, Columnist and Writer instead! Something that I had always aspired to and wanted as a kid – but knew my 'father would have killed me' metaphorically speaking – if he knew what was in the mind of his son then! For the rest of my life what he said to me I can never forget – though forgiven – when he abruptly said to me – Why should I help you? Tomorrow you will live in a posh area, drive a big posh car – and what will I get in return? You mocking and making fun at me?

Some years later – I never learn my lesson – a friend took me to his office for 'finding me a job – to pay off my bills' – and as soon as I had entered – and here the appointment was made in advance – he picked up the phone – and was telling the person at end of the other line – he is here now – he is looking for a job – but I will not help him! I guess he was so excited to 'fix me' that he did not know what he was really doing – or the evil side of him got better of him!  What hurt me more is not his words – but knowing whom he was talking at the other end. Though I too have forgiven – but the wound will never heal – and it is best to leave these things to Allah God only!

We are again talking of SMEs! But SMEs cannot stand late and delayed business payments – especially when it comes to postdated cheques! PDC – the famous that even the 'guys that do not speak any English know what it means! Including delayed car installments payments. Again it is Ramadhan – and Great Offers all coming up – but the person who was expecting his payments – and did not receive them in time – is exposed and in great danger of his personal freedom, movement and liberty – if he has taken such a car on installments – and he did not get paid in time!

The lapse and delay in some especially public places can go over 6 to 9 months even – but the PDCs cannot wait that long. Like I had said in my last week article – The Land Rover story – 'we have great ideas – but lousy not transparent implementation methods and systems – and not even ethical, not principled and not professional also! Unless these things really change on the grounds – we can all be given a copy of Animal Farm by George Orwell - as 'standard business manual to read – and keep!

When I was working in my last oil company – there was standard regulation that Suppliers and Invoices must be settled within 40 days – and it was implemented in the system as a follow up and counter check in the systems to follow. Yet in some of the places – even public places – you get excuses like 'we are very busy – but we will pay! Or the more annoying ones – the person in charge is away – for whatever reason – and we will follow up when he returns! Does this mean that if the person is away – no payments gets done? Why not recruit more Omanis? There are a lot of Omanis qualified out there still looking for jobs – or for changes and better prospects!

The sad and tragic part is that if payments are due to them and are delayed – especially the expatriate lots – poor fellows – get hit most! Even they can freeze their salaries – until they bring the monies in! No wonder they prefer expatriates to these jobs – but even them are now resisting – because the situation has simply gone overboard – and no one is accepting this anymore!

**I always believe this – it is far easier to destroy – and one smart aleck can destroy all the good works done by many for many years!**

**What more can I say now? Take Care!**

**By Majid Al Suleimany**

## B.13      Troubling and Complex Issues!
## A Review of One's Priorities!

**For Thursday – July 4th 2013.**

- *Character is simply habit long continued –* **Plutarch**

- *By the age of thirty, the character of a person has set like plaster – and will not soften again –* **William James**

There comes a time in one's life when things just get too complicated, difficult, perplexing and complex – and just do not get connected – and you have to move from one episode to another – and in utter and complete confusion in making any decisions of what is the best option out of the dire situation facing you! And whichever way you look at things and what to decide has, indeed, many pitfalls, issues and troubles – and could even result in personal harm and danger! You do not see the way out – and in front of you are only the trees – and you just cannot see the forest anymore now. There is the expression that perhaps you just do not do anything as a possible option – but that too you have to rule out! So then what do you really do?

There is also this point. Even if people know that on what you are complaining about has its legality, basis, authencity and validity – nobody wants you to say anything in your defense – and if you do – you are just wasting your time, efforts and energies – because nobody is going to listen to you. By opening your mouth, you remove all doubt! You end only in confirming the labels and colourings already made out for you – that you are simply trouble – and need to be avoided!

Even if they know deep down inside themselves – and even in hindsight, self-conscience and self-analysis - that you have a base and strong point to complain – and have all the valid and pertinent points – and need to be heard and attended to! This is the obstinate approach and outlook that leads to greater trouble and issues – but still people – even if knowing this – do not just care or bother! They remain as they are – and will just not change or adopt! And the more you try – the more they become withdrawn – and more obstinate and rigid – and even more harsh and punitive in retaliation!

The very same people will turn against you when things have really turned bad and sour – and they are caught in the middle – and heads are about to roll – and scapegoats are to be found – and that nobody has told them anything – and they know nothing of all these things – and it is the first time that they are hearing anyone telling them of these things! They are very good actors and impersonators – and may even switch roles to be the accusing type now – and abandon the defensive roles prior!

Human beings are supposed to be the most intelligent species on the globe – but they can easily disappoint and let you down – at the most inopportune time – when you really needed them to do otherwise!

Sometimes you feel that those people that just go along with things and are least bothered or caring may have the right approach in life – and are really more smarter and intelligent – because they have already analysed the situation – and have decided just to let things roll out as they are. They are least bothered – or care the least! Their only priorities and outlooks are – as long as I 'am not touched' - and can get what I want from the situation – I do not care about the rest of things! For them diplomacy is telling someone to go to hell – and he is looking forward for the trip!

In my columns – I have written many topics of the same theme and focuses – like Wasted Loyalties – Being Sincere in Life etc. If people do not even bother on the Religious books – do you think they will be bothered on what is written by human beings? People see things – hear things – people speak on these things to them – or they too may sometimes speak themselves – but that is all that is to it! Nothing more – nothing less!

It is always the people that do care and feel that get hit the most! And the more you are sincere, care and feel that you get more hit! You only end with a bloodied nose and swollen red head – by banging it against brick walls! In the end you become the bigger loser – nobody else!

You cannot change people - however hard you try! A leopard does not lose its spots – nor a tiger its stripes! And you cannot save someone – if he does not want it for himself! It is best to leave such people to their fate. As the saying goes – every dog has his day! So why intervene and interfere now – if you know all these things? A big question to ask yourself and only you can do this for yourself only! No one else can!

**Take Care!**

**By Majid Al Suleimany**

### B.15        The Girl Speaks!

**Malala Yousafzai at The United Nations!**

**For Thursday - July 14<sup>th</sup> 2013.**

- "I want education for the sons and daughters of all the Taliban and all the terrorists and extremists. I do not even hate the Talib who shot me. Even if there is a gun in my hands and he stands in front of me. I would not shoot him," Malala said.

-  "The extremists were, and they are, afraid of books and pens," added Malala - "They are also afraid of women."
- "Let us pick up our books and our pens. They are our most powerful weapons," Malala urged.
- "One child, one teacher, one book and one pen can change the world. Education is the only solution. Education first."

**I do not know if the speech was prepared for her** – or she had a hand or part in it – but for me - it was one of the most moving emotional speeches that I have heard for a very long time, indeed! One can only wish one had such as a daughter, niece – or younger sister! My eyes welled with tears from such a speech – and from such a young speaker – with defiant courage and stamina – and who had suffered so much in life! Left for dead after being shot by the Taliban – she rose up from the ashes – to where she is now! Speaking at the United Nations – in front of the whole world arena!

Malala Yousafzai celebrated her 16th birthday on the world stage at the United Nations, defiantly telling Taliban extremists who tried to end her campaign for girls' education in Pakistan with a bullet that the attack gave her new courage and demanding that world leaders provide free education to all children.

Malala was invited Friday to give her first public speech since she was shot in the head on her way back from school in Pakistan's Swat Valley last October. She addressed nearly 1,000 young leaders from over 100 countries at the U.N.'s first Youth Assembly — and she had a message for them too.

"Let us pick up our books and our pens. They are our most powerful weapons," Malala urged. "One child, one teacher, one book and one pen can change the world. Education is the only solution. Education first."

The U.N. had declared July 12 — her 16th birthday — "Malala Day." But she insisted it was "the day of every woman, every boy and every girl who have raised their voice for their rights." The Taliban, which has long opposed educating girls in Pakistan as well as neighboring Afghanistan, said it targeted Malala because she was campaigning for girls to go to school and promoted "Western thinking." The Boko Haram for Nigeria say the very same point too.

In what some observers saw as another sign of defiance, Malala said the white shawl she was wearing belonged to Pakistan's first woman prime minister, Benazir Bhutto, who was assassinated in December 2007 when she returned to run in elections. Malala recalled the Oct. 9 day when she was shot on the left side of her forehead, and her friends were shot as well.

She insisted she was just one of thousands of victims of the Taliban. "They thought that the bullets would silence us," she said. "But they failed. And then, out of that silence came thousands of voices. The terrorists thought that they would change our aims and stop our ambitions but nothing changed in my life except this: Weakness, fear and hopelessness died. Strength, power, fervour and courage was born."

Malala began her speech with a traditional Muslim prayer and later accused terrorists of "misusing the name of Islam and Pashtun society for their own personal benefits." She wore a traditional pink patterned South Asian dress and pants called a shalwar kameez and a matching head scarf.

Malala said she learned to "be peaceful and love everyone" from Indian independence leader Mohandas Gandhi and other global advocates of non-violence; from the compassion of religious figures Mohammad, Jesus Christ and Buddha; from the legacy of Martin Luther King, Nelson Mandela and Muhammad Ali Jinnah, who led Pakistan to independence in 1947.

Amid several standing ovations, Malala told the UN on Friday that the Taliban's attack had only made her more resolute. "I'm not against anyone, neither am I here to speak in terms of personal revenge against the Taliban, or any other terrorist group," she said. "I'm here to speak about the right of education for every child." Malala said her main focus was on the education. "There will be no compromise with any religious extremist who says girls should not go to school or stop going to school at 10." Today is for every woman, boy and girl raising their voice for human rights," she said in the speech.

Three million people have already signed a petition which Malala has presented to UN Secretary General Ban Ki Moon. Mr. Ban said: "In far too many places, students like Malala and their teachers are threatened, assaulted, even killed. "Through hate-filled actions, extremists have shown what frightens them the most: a girl with a book."

Malala's remarkable recovery has seen her become a high profile campaigner with her face being recognised all over the world. She was transferred to Birmingham in the UK and underwent extensive surgery to rebuild her skull at the Queen Elizabeth Hospital.

The UN event has been organised by former UK Prime Minister Gordon Brown, now the UN Special Envoy for Global Education. "This frail young girl who was seriously injured has become such a powerful symbol not just for the girls' right to education, but for the demand that we do something about it immediately," Mr Brown told CBS News.

UNESCO and Save the Children released a special reported ahead of Malala's speech. It found that 95% of the 28.5 million children who are not getting a primary school education live in low and lower-middle income countries: 44% in sub-Saharan Africa, 19% in south and west Asia and 14% in the Arab states. Girls make up 55% of the total and are often the victims of rape and other sexual violence that accompanies armed conflicts.

 Aid agencies say that female access to education in Pakistan is a particular problem. They say that the country ranks among the lowest in terms of girls' education enrolment, literacy and government spending. Youth campaigner Markson  Mwanza from Zambia told the Press : "There are a lot of myths in terms of persons with disabilities...that they can never achieve anything. "Looking what Malala has said it really brings hope to our lives, it brings hope to Zambia and all of us as people with disabilities."

**For a long time after this** - this speech will remain as the remnants of great speeches made in the world – and by great personalities. Malala has already been booked to write about her story – and highly paid too in millions of dollars. She is bound to be nominated aslso for the prestigious Noble Peace Prize – as the youngest contender ever! In trying to destroy her – the Taliban had created a great heroine instead – and given the world the answer to those that want to tarnish the name and image of Islam – to the extremeists – and to those determined in such tarnishing!

**Thank you Malala!**

**Take Care! Ramadhan Kareem!**

**By Majid Al Suleimany**

## B.16      The Telegraph Is No More!

### For Thursday - July 18<sup>th</sup> 2013.

**Where we  used to live as kids was this island off the main coast of Tanzania called Mafia** – from the famous Omani Arabic word of *'She Without'* – or locally known as Chole before the emigrating Omanis had named it as such! The reason was they were comparing this island with the bigger islands of what was once The Sultanate of Zanzibar – comprising the islands of Unguja and Pemba – and several others – and the eastern coasts of Africa – from Somalia to Mozambique as now! Mafia Island is about 120 kilometres south of the commercial capital city of Tanzania named Dar es Salaam – the city of peace – by Sultan Majid – the Zanzibar ruler then!

I was watching the mixed emotions of India closing down The Telegraph services as no more longer feasible and economical with the advent of the Internet, SMS and mobile phones (GSMs)! It reminded me of my youth days – where the only communication at the time with the outside world was the telegraph services – and even the radio to radio services sometimes did not work when there was bad weather and storms – which frequently hit the island! It would rain continuously day in and day out – for even 2 to 3 weeks unending and incessantly! My late father was a business person – shop keeper and transporter – and also as a plantation farmer – and many articles in my columns have been about this as kids!

In one of the funny anecdotes in India was this man sending a telegram to his son in UK – and it took 2 days to reach him there. The son was retorting to the father – why did you not send me an email – or a SMS message instead? And the father replying that 'old habits die hard – and I just did not think about it then'! In the olden days when you received a telegraph it was usually associated with bad news – that is why people dreaded most when one received a telegram! Though sometimes came in good news – like it is a boy! Or a girl!

In the place - there was this mysterious and weird strange Omani called 'The Bedouin'! Nobody knew who gave him or 'framed him' that name – except it stuck until his dying day when it was said loud for all to hear that Mr. Bedouin had died! He was a loner – a mysterious and keep to himself individual – and he used to scare some of us that he had magical and bewitching powers! He went to Africa alone – leaving all his family behind!

It was rumoured that he had 'magical powers' and he could fly at night all the way to our home town Hayll Al Ghaaf in Quriyaat – though originally our grandparents came from Manah! One day I teased him 'to teach me to fly with him' – and he retorted that 'you need to be really brave to be able to achieve such a feat' – when I teased him – M being M even as a boy! – that I wanted to see his magic carpet he flew at night times!

Seriously though, he would fly more during dates harvest times – and what he showed us was real fresh dates – but everyone was scared to 'try them' – and this made him more sad, lonely and miserable! I have not seen the dates myself – but my late elder brother - born in Oman - swore he did – and even ate some! Our poor late mother warned us to keep away from the person – but poor late dad with the usual S tribe sense of humour and wit – thought it all funny!

Coming to the point – one day this Bedouin came to the family shop – and called out loud – Said Nasser? (My father!) – *Come out here! I have bad news to tell you!* As most people had already discounted him already – anyway my father invited him in! But the man insisted for my father to come out to be seen visibly clear! Then he told my father – *Your Mother yesterday night had died in Oman – Allah Preserve our soul*! He repeated the message twice!

My late father – I could see his face turn all the colours – but there was still denial. Then he said to my father – *If you don believe me – please mark the time and day*. 40 days later the letter arrived from Oman – and it was all true and correct! At the time was the joke our late father had received an Express Telegram from Oman – but the joke died soon afterwards when the letter came! The letter was the confirmation that we needed to take the person more seriously – even if we refused to accept the ripening dates he brought back!

Another incident I remembered as a boy of 10, was losing the money for the telegram my late father was sending to the Income Tax department in the capital – thus a very important document! I was scared to tell my father – so I begged the Post Official *'that I will pay him one day' – but please send the telegram for now!* When I told him why I was so scared to tell my father the truth – he sent the telegram as requested – but he accompanied trembling me to my father to get the money – and 'not to scare your children that much – old man'! The money was never found – and even after frequent retracing of my steps from home to the Post Office per se!

Years later, when in the oil company as a young man – until the 1980s – we used to still use telegraphic messages and telegrams! As a HR Officer, I could send messages to especially UK – but also to The Netherlands and USA – Houston! And also receive messages! During duty week times,  I was able to get to read all the telexes that came in for the company – even confidential and oil related – and the 'coded' ones too! The power was calling the concerned parties for action – for 3 days every 3 months you got to act as the MD of the Company! Just imagine – all the power and so associated and related – just because of telegraphic messages then!

In the UK as a student then in the 1970s, you could dictate a telegram by the phone! So I was sending this telegram to our relatives in Dar es Salaam - Tanzania - but later we found out it was sent to Jerusalaam in Palestine instead! The pun was taken out as the message was very important at the time!

Like they say in life all good things do not last – and they have to end one day! But 'the Bedouin story' beats all odds and everything the telegram did – or was able to do! First of all - there were no telegrams then in the home town – and how, where and how you will address it – even if there were? Just imagine!

**Take Care! Ramadhan Kareem!**

**By Majid Al Suleimany**

# B.17        Insulting 'Relatives'!

## For Sunday - July 21st 2013.

**We are already moving towards the centre half of the fasting holy month of Ramadhan** - and as if we had just started fasting from yesterday – that is the blessings of the holy month for us all to see, recognise and admire! I watch the sermons after the Tarawih prayers in Mecca in Saudi Arabia – and the Priest calling for special duas and prayers for lots of suffering followers in different parts of the world – and sadly that some of them cannot even fast because of the wars of attrition and destructions – and the ensuing poltical and social upheavals in others. As the angels fly at night – they too may even cry – let alone human beings alone!

Today I want to concentrate on family problems and issues that may have already affected some of us – or possibly may affect others – if not already! As a small boy I used to be a loner and keep to myself – and those who have read my books or columns may recognise and remember that there were many unhappy and sad events and happenings in my life – not only serious and threatening – but nearly brought me to my early death and grave. You can find a good source from my article – The Glass Is Bent! – In my earlier website of **www.betweenusonly.com** or from my books!

In many of my columns articles, I have said the very same thing – in that after The Offices environments – there is no other place where people are most crude, abrupt and misbehave than in family relationships – ties, association and interfaces! I have noticed too when I wanted to make a list of people who have annoyed and upset me immensely for special treatment of learning hard and in difficulties to forgive in life – even if the forgetting part may take longer – or not at all. It can be very hard and difficult – but one must bring oneself to do so – because an 'eye for an eye' will end up in all being blind in the end! So what is the added value and advantage in this?

There is a famous Chinese expression that says – *If you are out to build a grave for your enemy – then dig two graves – and keep one for yourself!* Because in the ensuing fights you too may end as a casualty and fatality – and need the second grave too! Though I must admit it is not easy to do so, one must go for the high road – and there is no better example to copy and emulate than our own Great Prophet PBUH

---

When he rode victorious into Mecca – some of the people that had caused him great harm and injury came even from his own relatives and folks – but he did not retaliate – or take revenge from anyone – and that had ended in the growth and rise of converts to become Muslims – with some that went to other parts of the world to spread the word of Islam – from the very same people that waged war against it in the past!

As a young child – I was a boy that avoided fights with others – boys being boys! A few months before his death – my late father was observing and commenting to me on Eid day in my house – *I see all others getting continuous phone calls and messages – but you hardly receive any – poor M – like a child and still the same as an elder – no friends still!* He meant it in a very good way – but though the others took it wrongly that they were being complimented! That is the twists and ironies of life – and also its beauty and striking features in conversity too!

In our large family members there was bound to be some individual members that were aggressive and bullies to others – as their chosen patterns and behavior traits and characteristics. It is not a question of being a coward or being a weak person – but I always believed that in running away from such people – you avoid fights from their intrusive and penetrative behaviours to others – and you live to fight other battles in the future! I am trying my best to be witty here – and I do know that I am failing badly!

In the few and isolated cases that when I had decided to make a stand – and be ready for a fight – when all cautions and warnings prior have been ignored and passed the red lines – I was reprimanded that I was the eldest – and should show by example and deeds as the elder and leader – and not to get involved in the ensuing fights that were bound to happen!

This later part used to confuse and hurt me a lot – and as a kid I used to think that my parents did not like me – but they liked and preferred more The Aggressors than me! It took me a very long time to understand this – and The Puppy incident of following me to the mosque far years later made me understand and appreciate – as my late father was saying towards me – *That if you play with puppies – they will follow you to the mosque – because for the puppy it is just a building for them!*

Some years back, we had a relative from that distant land  - and who had stayed with us for quite awhile! We tried all our best to welcome them – and giving them the best that we could offer – and even going without and beyond too!

Like in most families there will always be these tell-tale family members – people that take pride and pleasures in causing rifts and divisions in people! The same peoples are very happy to see divisions and disasters between people – even if they are related and family. Some of them maybe from the same lots too! And that is the most sad and tragic part out of it all!

When I heard the tell-tale rumours - and being such a professional HR person whose first duty and prerogative is always to distinguish the wheat from the chaff – to come to the real truth and basis of things in life – I was shocked beyond belief to get so much hurtful, intrusive and aggressive responses from some of them – and what they had thought of our reception and welcome to them!

The ironical and tragic sad part was that when we went to visit them there before all these things – they had invited us for lunch – but in their own hours time – which was far away from our own time – and we were literally hungry as we ate the food – but had not complained to anyone – though they knew well in advance that our lunch times were not later than 2 pm

In life you try your level best! Whether it is reciprocated and appreciated or not is not important – and even if you get insulted in the process – but you did try – and gave it your best shot! There is a famous East African saying – *Do your good deed and proceed along – do not wait or expect any thanks or appreciation from anyone!* They are absolutely right – and fully agree!

**Take Care! Ramadhan Kareem!**

**By Majid Al Suleimany**

## B.18        Morsi: A Management Issue?

### Or more sinister forces at work and play?

For Wednesday 21ˢᵗ July, 2013

Outpoint – Before I start on the topic - I will try my level best to keep this article simple and apolitical – though I am still trying hard to understand and comprehend on what has really happened so far – and what possibly is now going to happen in the future – with all new 'Conspiracies Theories' emerging now!

In my article – Episode 14 – 'Advice To A New CEO' - dated August 27, 2003 in Book One – Between Us Only! – and over 10 years ago- I had said – Quote - .

The new CEO? Welcome Aboard! - …. But don't change a thing! - *The worst thing a new CEO can do is to sideline or marginalize those who have been actually running the establishment for many years (some very long plus 20 years!) and even before the CEO had joined. Key words are esteem, ethics, professionalism, esteem, respect and reciprocal good treatment!! And also leading by good examples and in leadership styles and practical demonstrations.*

Don't Change A Thing! - In its October 2002 issue, Harvard Business Review - HBR (Ideas with impact), noted famous Management Magazine notes the following in one of its topics - New CEO, Welcome Aboard (But Don't Change A Thing)"

➤ *"The folks at ……… were thrilled when they got a new CEO with fresh, bold ideas – until she started to act on them"*

➤ *(Old CEO to NEW) "Everyone here is in the slow lane. They are all wedded to the way things have always been done. You have to understand, this is a very old company. You may need to pull people along more slowly to make sure you don't end up tearing the place apart"*

> ➢ *"She (New CEO) – if she is not clear with this team, she'll be no better with the next. She should not make personnel (staff) changes until she has given the current team a chance.*

This is a commonly held Management Concept for Success for the CEO – (Leader) especially the new one! Refer to any Management expert or books on Management, the one fundamental advice that is always given to a new CEO or Official in joining an organisation, is never to 'rock the boat' on day one of joining! – However, good sincere and genuine your intentions may be!

In his book '7 habits of highly effective peoples', Dr. Stephen Convey, a Management 'guru', says that in addition of being  proactive and think win/win, 'it is very important to seek first to understand and then to be understood'. Others are Begin with the end in mind; Put first things first; Synergize, and sharpen the sword (socially, spiritually, physically & mentally).

'It is impossible for anyone to perform well in these continually changing roles without help from his subordinates in the organisation – he needs to have a well – informed objective understanding and supportive sounding board with whom he can freely discuss his doubts, fears and aspirations'.

- Robert L. Katz 'Skills of an Effective Administrator' – Three Skills Approach (Technical Skill, Human Skill and Conceptual Skills).

'The first duty - and the continuing responsibility of the Business Manager (CEO) are "to strive for the best possible economic results from the resources employed or available – by Peter F. Drucker – another Management guru.

There is nothing so bad and damaging than frustrated staff that suffer in disdain and in quiet, frustration, rancour, bitterness and in apathy and in disappointments. When staff are 'not healthy' the organisation also suffers eventually.  Productivity is affected.  You can forget ideas of expansion; survival of the establishment is highly taxed and put to great risks, deprivation and in detriment.

The concepts of Change Management are in itself complex in that even the Management do not agree to each other on what is the right approach and perspective to 'influence change' in itself per se. It is essential and vital to get everyone on board when contemplating and formulating changes. The underlying factor is that the new CEO especially has to understand and appreciate that he is dealing with the most complex of his resources - albeit it being the most paramount and important one too.

It is critical and extreme too if these changes would incorporate drastic changes or reversals in peoples entrenched formal positions - worse in informal leadership positions! - or their continued existence in the Organisation -  that the new CEO (Leader) uses all his tact, interpersonal and managerial skills to see participation and involvement of all the staff - or majority at least -  in these envisaged changes per se.

It is very important to make people working under you to feel that no particular polarization or group is being targeted in these changes, even if the intentions maybe good sincere and genuine, and this was 'not in the plans' per se! My advice and counsel to CEOs and 'the new man in Charge' is that not many of our subordinates are ready to take a risk to tell you exactly what they think or feel – especially when they see very bad and raw treatment vetted out on the long serving staff. You also need to always realize that whatever the good intentions you may have – there will be people 'dead set against you' – waiting for you to make the first mistake – before they jump on you!

It is not a question of just getting rid of only old staff who perhaps may be truly 'transfixed and rigid in their outlooks and approaches, or even 'dead wood' for that matter. It is a question of how you get to know the establishment well first, to get to know its social culture and its environment and modus operation, and how you tackle the issue and convince people.

The thing is called "tact" and the right and correct approach and how equitable, ethical and right approach and cohesion is taken.  Key words are esteem, ethics, professionalism, esteem, respect and reciprocal good treatment!! And also leading by examples and in demonstrations.

This is my (humble) advice to any CEO (Leader) who wants to make a niche and name for himself, and to be acknowledged as a 'successful CEO (Leader)' – and not a loser (and either be sidelined / marginalized or even eventually be jobless or to be routed out even - because what goes around, comes around!

Remember you are the driver of the car, when your passengers are scared, they will not tell you of the obstacles you cannot see. You will only see after inadvertently you have hit them! That is the worst-case scenario for any CEO! New or Old! You can find the full article in my www.majidall.com

The rest is history on what has happened to Morsi. A lot of 'Conspiracy Stories' are now emerging as to why he was removed from power – including The Ethiopian Dam Link – The Israeli-Saudi link – and the usual of The West not wanting an 'Islamic Government' to succeed in Egypt – after The Turkey and Senegal experiences etc – and 'refusing to accept 'Democracy results' in previously Algeria and Gaza.

Anyway, as I had promised in the beginning I will stop here – as my usual style in writing of 'taking you up to the bridge – and then letting you decide if you want to cross it – or go back.

This article is dedicated to the innocent lost lives and maimed ones in the 'unneeded and unwanted called for' massacres – instead of following our Religion and The Hadith in solving our own problems our own ways – by frank honest sincere genuine one-to-one – give-and-take – face2face discussions – and in making hard, difficult complex decisions for compromises, settlements and solutions.

Praying for our Egyptian brothers – and May Allah Guide us and Protect and Preserve us all from His Anger and Fury – Amin

With sincere and due apologies,

By:

Majid Al-Suleimany

Date - August 19, 2013

## B.19          The Pain Inside!

### For Wednesday August 28th 2013

- *A mirror shows the outside, but never the pain on the inside! –* **Anon**
- *Turn your wounds into wisdom! –* **Oprah Winfrey**

*The Pain Inside* **is an** *Al Jazeera Television World* **series programme. Al Jazeera explains -** After military service, many young Israelis travel abroad to distance themselves from distressing experiences. In Israel, military service is compulsory for most people over the age of 18, with men serving three years and women two. Exemption from military service is a hotly debated issue in Israeli society. Many feel that military service is a matter of family obligation and loyalty to their 'homeland' For some, joining the army is about the connections they make. Some employers also hesitate to recruit Israelis who refuse to serve in the army.

Following their army stint, tired and stressed, thousands of ex-soldiers travel to India and elsewhere to party and hang out with each other - it is a rite of passage for many. As Israelis do not need a visa to enter Europe so many young Israelis also emigrate to cities in Europe, such as Berlin. Nowadays, around 30,000 of them live in Germany's capital, many having chosen to leave all the restrictions and constraints of life in Israel behind.

Other Israelis become conscientious objectors, these are people who say they understand what the word 'occupation' really means, and therefore refuse to serve in the Israeli military. For many, life in Israel - with its military conscription and occupation - is turning young people into what one Israeli interviewee describes as "monsters in a distorted reality", revealing deep psychological issues which remain unaddressed.

There is a sense of a lost generation - of people who are deeply troubled and alienated from their own humanity. People talk of living in a "bubble" in Tel Aviv and the future of Israel "hanging by a thread". The film reveals this agitation in Israel, at times manifesting itself through exodus, which is the very opposite of the Zionist dream.

- *We live in the Middle East but we refuse to accept the fact that we are part of it. I think this pretty much indicates that there is an identity crisis in Israel –* **a Gabriel Moses, exempted from military service**

**In my Book One – Between Us Only! Article - 'Lost Blood'** – I recall the incident of my first encounter with one Israeli boy – a Diplomatic student in the High School I used to attend in that distant land.  Quote - That ended the friendship, though the day he left he took my address. I never expected to get any response from him.

Years later he sent me  a  small  note  in the same place – it just said  -  *Thank you for trying to make me feel welcome and as a friend! I still remember your words. I hope one day I can invite you to my country and there will be peace amongst our peoples and that we can be Real First Cousins!*

In my holiday stay in a hotel in Zanzibar a few years back – I was approached by this sort of 'foreign Arabic' looking pretty girl asking about a certain place she and her friends wanted to visit – thinking I would know the place as I was speaking the local lingo to the hotel staff. When I told her I do not know the place – she was very much surprised till I explained that I came from Oman. She then said to me – *So you are Arab?* I said – *I think so! In that case* – she retorted – *Then I should not be speaking to you!. Because I am Jewish!* The last part was in perfect Arabic.

So I replied - *I think conversely – because we are cousins – and should be talking to each other! That is a new one* – she retorted - *I will tell all my friends back at home on this!* She and her parents actually originally came from Yemen! She too was in the 'The Pain Inside' group – and narrated to me how she had helped a Lebanese old woman during the Lebanese invasion. The shock on the old woman's face was not the war – but 'the uniform she was wearing'!

When I was a young boy and during the colonial times in that distant island – the District Commissioner then used to speak in Arabic to my late Father. This surprised the locals very much – until they came to realise that his origins were also Jewish!

In my latest book Wipe My Tears! – **www.myownmajid.com** – I said - *The book also carries many family, offices and human based articles that are applicable to us all - as bottom line we are the same human being in that same a person – with the same needs, wants and fears - devoid of race, religion, creed and colour! Many of the articles are highly emotive and heart rendering – and that is the reason of adopting the title of Wipe My Tears!*

**Some more 'The Pain Inside' Footnote sayings: -**

- *Numbing the pain for a while will make it worse when you finally feel it* – **J. K. Rowling**

- *Life is a pain! Anyone who says differently is selling something else –* **William Goldman**
- *Tragedy should be utilized as a source of strength –* **The Dalai Lama**
- *There are wounds that never show on the body that are deeper and more hurtful than anything that bleeds –* **Laurel Hamilton**
- *One thing that you cannot hide is when you are crippled inside –* **John Lennon**

**Take Care!**

**By: Majid Al-Suleimany**

Date - August 26, 2013

**B.20          Things Have Not Really Changed!**

**People Are Just Still Misbehaving!**

**For Sunday August 25th 2013**

**Things Have Simply Not Really Changed!**

- *Do not bite the hand that feeds you – to end licking the boot that will kick you!*

- *Maybe you should consider our place. Here we do respect the learned elders like you!* – My Books USA Publishers.

**Thursday – August 15th 2013.**

**This week I had tried my level best** – and avoided to get embroiled into an argument with one – sorry to say it to those of my friends! – An Indian Top Sales Marketing guy – a Services Provider that I have been using for a number of years. Related to my books distribution in Oman, I have given them good business in the past – and the relationships were to mutual advantages, anyway!

There is no point to continue banging my head against brick walls – and just making it swollen and red in the process! Five years ago, I had formally reported this same guy to his Indian Superiors – and I went so far to report him formally to The Company Owners – who are Omanis – acknowledged and well known family run business. But instead of siding with the customers – and fellow Omanis – they tend to side more with their own staff – even if rude and misbehaving ones too - like this one too!

The person promised to change and behave – but simply has not!  He just feels that he is beyond reproach – and nothing can touch him in any way! One would be even excused to think that he may be doing the 'company's dirty business' under the cloak and face mask! In treating even qualified, experienced and professional Omanis with complete disdain and contempt. The mind just boggles of how he treats the Junior Younger Omanis under him.

These kind of things lead to bigger things – as we have seen lately live on television. The other day I was seeing this traumatic depressing television news coverage of a young Syrian girl of about 5 years of age - desperately gasping out 'I am alive' – leave me alone – unsaid! - As she wanted to cover herself from prying television cameras. It was so distressing and disheartening – to see how fast the girl could grow up in such nasty awful experiences. We see these things – do we change? The answer is simply – No! Until the next time – if there will be such a chance then!

I then told the person that I am collecting back all my books still with you – and please keep them ready for my collection. What is the use and point, anyway? I have written two books in Management in these issues –
**http://www.myownmajid.com** – and several column articles before! I do not know how long these things will continue – before there is a breaking point? Perhaps it may come sooner than what we had envisaged! People should not be surprised in this!

In my book theme – A Cry For Help! – Published in 2009 – I had said – Addressing the increased extremism, fundamentalism and lack of forbearance in the working environments.... Growing radicalization of local staff.....Unhappy dissatisfied staff ....bad treatment of staff – especially by some (few) expatriates ....etc.! My mistake forgetting to add ...and customers and clients too!

Truthfully and honestly sincerely speaking - the problems with us Omanis are that we are very welcoming, respecting and esteeming to 'The Invited Guests' in our country – unalike even others near us! The few of them especially feel it is okay for these unruly unneeded behaviours and attitudes – and to in forgetting the famous expression – Biting the hand that feeds you ...and ending as proved in many cases – of 'licking the boot that kicks you'!!

I am not a Political Scientist or Expert – but since last week I have never ever felt so sad in my life ever before – because all the things I have said and cautioned about have come to pass – and I feel so sad, unhappy and miserable to keep saying – I have said it, before! Or I told you so! I tried to say the very same things - diplomatically and tactfully – in my many articles – notably last month – *The Role of Advisors!* The article can be found here!

Even at the dangers of losing something so nice and good that you had never had before or expected – and something you should strive to protect, defend and let it grow and prosper – the evilness and selfishness in people will just not change – even if they know their actions – or inactions – would lead to what, where and when!

I have worked in other countries in GCC – and I have met many ex worked in Oman expatriates. Though they are getting 'better salary packages, perks and benefits than what they got here – the one thing that they miss the most – is the 'warm welcome and esteem' that expatriates – the so-called 'invited guests' – have got in Oman. This particular aspect they missed the most.

Frankly, I have seen it live too being practiced - the opposite of what we Omanis are doing! In my role of Human Resources – I had even protested in 'defending and protecting' schemes – and I was rudely and abruptly awakened by those doing these things against the expatriates – *Brother – you are not in Oman now!* That speaks volumes of what we offer and give here – to say the very least! It eventually even costed me my job!

The main problem is that some expatriates know very well that they will not get the positions and levels they are in now – if they were back at home! They may try to kid and fool – but they are fooling no one – but themselves more! I keep repeating and stressing the word FEW! This definitely has gone to their heads – and have made them contemptuous, proud and conceited. That is the sad and bitter truth of the matter – human beings as they are in reality!

Conversely, I do not know what we Omanis may do – if we enmasse are to go and work in high influential positions in other places? How we would react, interface and behave? As Bishop Desmond Tutu was saying to Sir Robert Frost in the interview – *I do not hate the individuals who propagated, promoted and practiced Apartheid – because as an African – I do not know what their minds were really thinking? Perhaps if I was one of them – I could be doing the same – or maybe even worse!* Wise words, indeed!

**May Allah God Protect and Preserve us all – from His Anger and Fury – Amin.**

**With sincere and due apologies,**

**By:**

**Majid Al-Suleimany**

**Date - August 23, 2013**

## B.21    Expatriate Casual Workers!
### For Sunday September 1st 2013

**I was reading this news headline** (Muscat Daily August 29th 2013) titled 'Municipality faces shortfall of workers' – 'Many decide to leave because of new contract system'!  It seemed that many of the workers are now going to get reduced salaries and without allowances – and those who used to get up to OMR 260 per month – depending on their grades – are now going to get average of 150 per month!

Frankly and honestly speaking, sometimes the mind just boggles who actually makes such decisions that subsequently leads to such results and consequences – and whether the decisions were well thought and considered before thoroughly prior to make such random and hasty decisions?

In an article I had written on the same subject – over 10 years ago – I had said – These jobs (Municipality Cleaners) would be the last jobs to be Omanised – and even far after the last Expatriate CEO and Manager have left the country! These casual jobs have better future prospects than even the Management ones of their peers. I went on – At 3 a.m. they are still cleaning the streets – whilst the rest of us all are snoring deeply in our beds!

Some years back - I was travelling one night at 4 am to pick a visitor at Muscat Airport - and I nearly witnessed a 'nasty road accident' - when one of the Cleaners had moved towards half of the road to pick up a tissue left on the road – and the poor man was nearly run over by a speeding car – even at this late hour in the empty road. I do not know what the rush was in for?

There are no takers for these jobs. I am frankly convinced that our youth would prefer to live 'on social welfare' - as a worst case scenario – then go and do these jobs! A long time ago some people had come to deliver a washing machine to my villa in Qorum. This is what I had written in my article – quote – The Angry Driver – He (the young Omani youngster) nearly ran over me as he was reversing the truck fast as I was guiding him through the gate. I asked him what gives? Or should I call the Police? He broke down saying that this job (truck driver) was the only job he could get!

So I asked him – Forgive me Son! What qualifications do you have? He said he did not even finish his final secondary school! Madam wife was annoyed why I was getting involved – when I told him bluntly that he should thank his 'lucky stars' that he got a job! The young boy turned to his Indian peers saying in their lingo – These rich people look down on us – because we are poor! Yes I live in Qorum – thanks to my Oil Company – but I am certainly not rich! I could not hold back my laughter – because he did not know that I studied in Tanzania in Indian Schools from Class 1 Primary to High School! At young age I could even write my name – and my father's – in Hindi – and embarrassing the boy even further!

At another occasion in another place there was an elder Omani with some Indian workers. When he saw me 'he was guiding the other workers' – and I had thought that he was the 'foreman' – but he had elected himself for the position. The real foreman (Indian) soon put 'the show off' man 'right back to his position'!

When I studied in UK I stayed in a house belonging to a Pakistani. He came to UK and though had some certificates ended as a bus driver! He had saved enough to be able to get himself a house in the end! Even if after a shift – if there was no other driver in the other shifts – or not turning up – as in many cases – especially in weekends and immediately afterwards – he would volunteer – and he used to get double rate for going extra shift! His local peers had all their monies go into bars and girl friends!

We should also remember – in conclusion – that the basic salaries for Omani Youth had gone up. This is a wrong time to reduce their salaries (expatriates) human beings as they are in 'comparing and contrasting'!

**As a Human Resources Professional of over 35 years** – and Management Consultant, Expert and Advisor  for over 12 years – I think a review is in order – under all the aforementioned  - and with due and sincere apologies!

**Take Care!**

**By: Majid Al-Suleimany**

**Date - August 26, 2013**

## B.22            Are You A VIP?

### A growing trend that needs to be nipped in the bud!

### For Sunday September 8th 2013

- *Never take a person's dignity; it is worth everything to them - and nothing to you!* - Frank Barron

**Believe me but I am a very respectful person** – and I always greet elders to me – VIP or not – with the greatest level of respect, esteem and affection! I give them the highest level of patience, tolerance and respects that I can muster. When I greet anyone - I offer both hands in salutation and greetings – just like a kid to a grown up! I even slightly bow my head – especially if an elder is involved! That is how I was brought up in life – and I do the same pass on teachings and preaching to my children – and the grandchildren.

But I am also a give and take type of person – live and let live! The other day my granddaughter was lamenting loudly for all to hear – Grandfather always is confusing! Sometimes he has too much hair on his head- sometimes he shaves clean! This after seeing me lose all my hair! So the others laughed nervously – whilst all the time looking at me how I will react – and I was sincerely laughing the loudest! Believe me!

I respect one speaking his or her mind – myself being a victim of such circumstances all around in my life.  If in the old days I tried to joke this to my late grandfather, I would get slaps from different sources – and for 'insulting grandfather' - and yet Grandfather would still say – 'I am not amused'!

I do not know if you have noticed it? I can make exceptions if it is a wedding – but certainly a funeral gathering is a different thing and place! It is not a place to pull rank – and or show your credentials to others in life!

One time at a wedding of a friend I was sitting near a VIP. And to start idle polite chat I asked him where he was working? And the good man – diplomatically and politely – replied at a certain Ministry. I had the guts and audacity to criticise the place. He seemed to want to know more – so I gave it to him!

All the time I could see his face trying hard to hide his smirking face – and the shock was mine when I got a call few days later – I had given him my card! I was told 'you talked to HE' at the wedding – and I am looking at your case!

A few days later a friend casually remarked to me – Did you know whom you were talking to there then? I said No! Don't you read the newspapers? See TV? I hope you did not say anything off point? Off point? What do you mean? I have met very high VIPS – yet they are very simple people – and conversely it is they that make you feel relaxed and comfortable! That is the beauty of Oman! A beacon of light and hope to others all around us!

The problems we have are with the second and third class Actors and Performers! Believe me – I am not a jealous envious person by nature – or try my best not to! A few baizas added in their dishdashas or dresses – a few job levels upwards – and they look at you with squinted eyes and with disdain and contempt! We are better than you! We are more important than you! Are you a VIP? No? So move along! Move away! Go away from me! Move!

The worst offenders are the Organisers and the administrators! Actually self-made! Self-proclaimed! Nobody has appointed them to these positions! Like I have said before – I can accept and allow exceptions in weddings! We like it or not – that is how the cookie crumbles! You can never change human attitudes and behaviours! Either you have it – or you do not!

There is no middle ground – or exception? Or like I always like to quote – The Third Option! But for heaven's sake – even at funeral gatherings – there is a class division? When someone has just died? The same worms will eat and devour you – whether you are rich or poor! They do not know any distinction and or difference! Food is food for them! Sorry to be morbid!

The other day I met this person. I introduced myself to him with great smiles, warmth and sincerity! First time I have ever met him vis-à-vis – face to face! I would not declassify him as not a VIP! But if you look at things some way people look at things – even poor me could be a VIP? One man's VIP is another's Loafer! Or lower level type of guy! If there is such a thing!

He was just casual – The Ahlaan (Welcome) was more polite as others at the funeral were around! There was no attempt to say more – or pull me to stay near him! Anyway, he was busy talking to someone near him – perhaps a Real VIP! I felt myself like wanting to sink into the ground – more when the Organisers – having checked the facts – realised I was No VIP – so let me go to the end of the sitting arrangement scats end! No one came to pick me to me to the centre – or to the nearby aisles! I was not VIP! So why bother?

Next time I will think twice to go to a funeral gathering especially – unless I know well the died person  – and or family! When my father died – and when my mother died – I did not see any of even the sorts of VIPs I knew at the gathering – 2 or 3 sent only emails and SMS! I was not VIP! But yet at their family members' funerals – I had cancelled everything to attend!

**The East Africans say** – Those who go up the ladder will have to come down! Or Be nice to the person going up – because you will meet him coming down! – East African famous!

**Take Care!**

**By: Majid Al-Suleimany**

**Date – September 6<sup>th</sup> 2013**

## B.23          The Sob Stories!

A growing trend that too needs to be nipped in the bud!

For Wednesday September 11th 2013

- Whoever abstains from asking others for some financial help, Allah will give him and save him from asking others, Allah will make him self-sufficient – **Al Bukhari**
- Abu Huraira related that the Prophet had said: He who makes a habit of asking from others reaches out for a brand of Fire, so let him refrain or continue, as he desires – **Muslim.**
- *Give a man a fish and you feed him for a day – Teach a man to fish and you feed him for a life time* – **Chinese Saying.**

In one of my earlier articles a few years ago – I wrote about this incident that had happened to us in the family after returning to the place we had left – and after the Zanzibar Revolution. Our uncle had been hosting us in his house to stay – which originally was our own house before - arriving there broke and penniless! Food was an issue due to depleted funds – and in one of the meals I had casually remarked – being a novice young boy without thinking properly – that I had enjoyed the food as being half hungry!

My late father was visibly upset in 'forgetting myself and in embarrassing the family per se'! He sadly lamented to me – we come from a proud stock  and branch – and we do not stoop low or degrade ourselves in front of others – even if excusably that we are hungry and in need! Keep your head high – and these are tests from God – and we will overcome – and win!

Remember this always – my son! And that was my late father's outlook and philosophy – though he rode the same donkey in Oman to school with others that later came to be very high VIPs! He had never in his life approached them for anything – and even if they had asked him if we needed anything – he would reply strongly steadfastly that 'we were okay – thank you for asking!'

One time at a shopping complex, I saw this old banger type of car – which speaks volumes of the expatriate driver of the car – he half clutched and abruptly started off the car – when he saw me approaching him! I followed him to the flat he was staying – and asked him why did you do that? His response was - I thought you were coming to beg some money from me 'with a sob' story – like many I have met at this place! So I told him off – all I wanted to tell you was you had your full lights beam on – being day time anyway! As he was apologising profusely – I decided to leave him – before I gave him 'a real piece of my mind'! That is how low we the locals have stooped on – to vet such treatment – even from peoples that 'have millions of beggars' back at home!

During the month of Ramadhan we had women with children tailing behind them with all kinds of sob stories. The new trend is from Syria – but what boggles the mind is how they have entered the country – if they were real and genuine cases! It reminds me of the Arabic comedy scene of (Professor) Ghawar – asking the border police in the scene – why he was 'not asking the goats' crossing the border 'for their passports'?

A friend of mine was telling me of one particular lady who had a difficult misbehaving son – who was causing her tremendous woe and troubles by his behaviours – even to his wife and children. The boy was terminated jobless with the same crude behaviour and attitudes at work! His wife had left him – taking the children with her. The poor mother was suffering terribly and a lot – mothers being mothers! Even if she knew deep down about her son! The poor lady was going from house to house to collect money to pay for the escapades of his son – perhaps even drugs related too!

Believe me, I am a softie for such sob stories – and I am caught many times that too late I have been scammed and duped - and have been fooled again! I asked a Religious Person once – he said to me – if you have the money and you want to help – just do it. You are not responsible for 'the sins that the person is getting for hoodwinking others' – that is not your responsibilities – but his alone! Some of them have even x-rays of why 'they are disabled, invalid and incapacitated! Unless you are in the Medical profession – you just have to believe what you see!

When we came back to Oman in the early 1970s – this trend was not there – and even in isolated cases if there were – it was very tiny and minute – not like now 'where is the fashion and trend – of getting fast and easy money from gullible and unsuspecting lots. And even if they were a bit suspicious – they still give for peace and conveniences – and seeing the 'poor children's eyes of desperation and need'!

What makes me worry a lot and be concerned – is perhaps we are 'turning away real and genuine' cases of need and want – by being overzealous sceptical and suspicious! I recall personally an incident of a taxi driver whose car had run out of petrol on the road. I was the only one who had stopped. And the few Rials I gave him - I gave more as 'sadaka' – alms – but the shock was on me and my sneering sarcastic staff the next day – when he brought a big plate of halwa and his farm produce – 'because you were the only person who had stopped, trusted and helped me!

**My books and my columns have many such kind of stories! Take Care!**

**By: Majid Al-Suleimany**

**Date – September 6th 2013**

## B.24          The Sealed Fates in Life!

### For Sunday September 15th 2013

**After more than 10 years from the last time I had visited** - this week I had the pleasure and the privilege to visit again The Oman Daily Observer Offices and meet some of my new and the usual old friends there!

In my first visit I was being interviewed for the start of the 'infamous' Between Us Only! column. It is a wonder and strange thing to notice that many of the people we meet nowadays seem to have so aged – and so tired and forlorn – as if they have learnt to 'give up and just accept their fate' – and that there is simply nothing that they can do now to look at things anew and afresh - change their path – but to go on as before! Nothing has changed that much! Human nature and habits are just like that – and nothing has gone amiss!

I look at the newspaper delivery boy. I ask him how many years he has been doing the same job – day in and day out - and whether he has any other plans for his remaining days on earth – and he retorts – sadly and sarcastically – what else can I do but sell newspapers? He continues - Even I had to learn how to drive a motorcycle first before I could do the job! I have had my hands broken twice by a car hitting me from behind – because the way people drive – they just cannot accept a motor cycle to occupy the 'space of a car' in front of them! So the many cases when he had to pull sharply right – for safety's sake!

I had my hair cut at the saloon. Here is another profession. All he knows is to cut hair - since a young man at 16. 30 years later he is still cutting hair – but not in his country – but in a different country! Even here he has to fight to keep his job – with constant checks and inspections. Yet they still want the jobs for their own young men – but there are no takers! Though you would think that people would be happy that there is someone out there that is 'willing and keen' to do the job even! The same case for the sandwich (shawarma) boy! The drivers – especially the heavy duty ones! The mechanics! The Municipality cleaners! You name it!

But it is not only the expatriates – it is the locals too! The same clerks, PROs, the secretaries, the bank staff, the drilling jobs, the stewards and stewardess, the airline crews – you name it! Not all of them can get 'lucky breaks' in life – like the admin clerk I know who looked that smart, intelligent and promising – and picked out to go for an academic course overseas – takes engineering – and becomes an Engineering Director!

Those he left have also moved forward – but the luckier ones to an officer or supervisor level at the most! Suppose the said clerk had refused to go for the course – would he have remained in the same lots – or would still fate tempt him to a faster lane – in another route? Your guess is as good as mine!

My Literature Teacher in Secondary School in Tanzania – that pretty Miss F – then and probably is still – told me – M – Life is like a drama. You are given a role in it – and all you can do is play your role well! She had a thing for me – she liked me a lot! Years later after I had left the place – she had returned back home to Goa India! I was just wondering out loud what she would be doing back at returning home – even if married now – if not only as a Teacher?

I had then a working peer sitting opposite me in the oil company. Every pay day he would come to my office and lament – this salary is just not enough! Smart I would retort – Be thankful – there are people out there receiving far less in life – and some not at all. He even suggested we go into business together – but the idea of business just scared me then!

I should have stayed with my gut feelings – and had never gone into business – and end going bust! But my friend made it – he became rich and successful! Those he left behind? Of course they moved up too – 2 or 3 job levels up! The great man has even offered jobs to the same peoples – even those who were 'more senior to him' at the job front!

What do you say to the 'bus driver' who has ended up to be a President of a country – after entering politics? Or the boat man? Or Great Late Margaret Thatcher – drawing attention to herself - 'that she was just a shopkeeper's daughter'!

Yet still - in one of my local flights in that distant place – I had met the ex President – no longer in high position – though there were 1 or 2 people 'still looking after him'. Maybe I was staring at him too much – so he smiled and came over to me! Believe me - him coming to me? I think I was bumbling and getting confused –

because this was the same 'personality' that we stood on the road sides cheering as his motorcade went past! Now we were in the same flight – all the seats were economy class! So many cases like him – no longer in high offices of power! Simple people back again!

The other day in the Masjid I went to greet this great personality. So I said to him – I guess you will not remember me? But you had given our family a good and great picnic meal one time! I tried to remind him. The good tired forlorn man looked at me with sad eyes – You remember a meal? I did greater things to others – they do not even bother to even speak to me – let alone come and greet me like you did. So I should say Thank You – Not you!

**As the Brits say** – that is how the cookie crumbles! Or the great words of Miss F – and there is nothing more that you can do about it! You are telling me? Remember me? I did try – but sometimes you just have to accept that 'your fate is sealed in life' – if even moving to writing as a substitute - can be called that too!

**Take Care!**

**By: Majid Al-Suleimany**

**Date – September 13th 2013**

# B. 25          The Marriage Proposal!

From The Pampers To The Wedding Dress!

For Wednesday September 18th 2013

*If friendship is your weakest point then you are the strongest person in the world* – **Abraham Lincoln**

**There is something quite definite about our (late) parents** that though they are not that highly educated – but they are more smart, intelligent and wiser than what we are – and ever hope to be in life! As time goes by – the graph will only take a more dip downwards than the status quo!

Long time ago – when I was showing the plot and drawings of my villa in Qorum Heights – the small villa but with the big heart – my late father was lamenting that he does not see a spare bedroom in the sketch! So I asked him – what for dad? You mean for the guests? No – he sadly lamented – just in case for one of your daughters – if she decides to return home!

Though they are not really for us – to be with us forever - still the daughters are our responsibilities – even after long they have got married – and have children too! Then I recalled the incidents when my late sister used to come back home – and nobody had asked her anything – until she was cooler and calmer – and now was ready and wanted to talk! A few days she herself would return to her husband – on her own too!

One of my friends and peer at work at one time had invited me to the coming wedding of his son. As we sat talking – he was lamenting to me that if you do not learn from others experiences – then God will teach you instead! So I could see the man was highly stringed and troubled – and wanted to talk! So I prompted and encouraged him to go on and to do so!

So the poor man broke down – and he narrated to me that his son was going to get married to an offspring that came out of two groupings of people that – putting it rather mildly – he was 'not too keen with'!  That is God's mysterious ways of giving you Life's Teachings! The man used to boast to me how in his job pursuits he used to make 'special attention' to these two groups – and where it would go on okay with anyone else – but with the exception of them!

A great sign of great leadership is seeing something with your own eyes – and you acting upon it immediately afterwards. It is said that the Great Prophet PBUH was passing one day – and he heard a woman singing sadly  to herself that she was 'missing her husband' - who had gone off to the wars then!  So a rotation system was introduced instead – to bring some of the men back home!

This happened to me too this week! I was outside the housemaid room – and I thought I heard crying! So next morning – as diplomatically and tactfully that I could muster – I asked her – what gives! Bear with me for awhile – but it will be clear at the end of this article – as to why the poor lady was crying too!

Anyway – this week I had received a 'high powered' delegation coming to ask for 'the hand of my last daughter! Like any other father – I was torn between seeing her go away from the home – and seeing that my daughter was moving on with her life – and after starting work on completion of her Engineering Degree in the UK! For a girl to take such a field – and to be able to work in the desert locations – is in itself a great example and demonstration how far ahead and developed Oman has become now!

With people reporting to her – who were all 'born and bred' males – but modernity had caught up with us! As a person in HR – I recall many incidents of the so-called 'stout and strong minded real men' - who had refused to formally report to the fairer sex – until and unless the 'books were thrown' at them! Those were our old ways – we now have even their Excellencies the Ministers too!

They say the world is a small place – because you never know whom you will meet later in life – or need from that someone! Even if you think that you are rich and powerful – and 'nothing can ever touch you' – as in the last week's article – The Sealed Fates in Life! You may think someone is insignificant and unimportant – and then you are forced to eat your own words – whether by mitigating circumstances and or by nature itself! Whether you like it or not – because events and fate have caught up with you now – and you are just helpless and impotent!

So I had a long chat with the Filipino housemaid. Then she told me – Oh Pappa - I came to Oman when MM was only one year old – today she has blossomed to be a fully-fledged woman (girl) – and getting married too! From changing her pampers – to now assist her in wearing a bridal dress! How time flies – she sadly lamented! You know Pappa? Your above article last week made me think a lot – like many of your articles do!

My late father used to watch his grandchildren – and great grandchildren play! He used to ask us – Do you think they will remember and know each other (in the future)? So I used to tease back – Of course they will! You must be joking – my father sarcastically hit back – if even their parents 'do not know each other now' – how do you expect their children – and grandchildren – to remember! My later father never minced his words – calling 'a spade a spade'!

I wished the old man was around – because he would see his granddaughter getting married now – and I will be keeping the room for her – just as he had advised! Though I am trying hard to resist in the temptation to convert it into an office – because I now use the dining room as also an office – books take a lot of the space - and the 'friction cause and strife' with Great Madam Wife – GMW – especially when guests are invited! Just gathering storm clouds – and for more storms coming ahead – unless I can get some money quickly now – for a much needed break! I have never been on a holiday break for the last 5 years!

My granddaughter was then saying to us – so Aunty MM is getting married now? Soon she will have babies – and what will they call me? We just look at her in 'shock and awe' – especially seeing she is just 5! Who is teaching them these things? Where do they learn such things? The mind just boggles....! Gets scarier and scarier – by the day!

**Take Care!**

**By: Majid Al-Suleimany**

**Date – September 13<sup>th</sup> 2013**

## B.25            The Open Letter!

### A Letter From My Heart!

For Sunday September 22nd 2013

**Day before yesterday evening (Monday September 16, 2013) I had cut my left palm – just a little bit –** with a sharp knife whilst cutting some oranges! The scare and shock was more for me to see so much blood coming out from my hand! But that was not alone and enough – I just attended to myself using the First Aid experiences I knew – till the blood had stopped spurted out! Only then I told the members of my family! Funnily, I did not want to disturb anyone – and let the family members at the house continue doing whatever they were doing uninterrupted – whilst I dealt with my case on my own time and volition.

After the blood had considerably stopped – I then told them – showing them the bloodied tissues! My daughter in law T then applied plaster and bandage – and the blood then stopped completely!

It is not a question of making mountains out of molehills – but I was wondering to myself why I did all these things on my own – rather than involving my family? Frankly – I did not want to disturb them – and I remember a late very good friend of mine who had cautioned me – M? You may be surrounded by a lot of family and others – but yet be the loneliest person on the face of the earth – and suffer alone and in silence.

This poor man had died later on since early morning by a heart attack – but his wife and family were away – and it was only late evening when the houseboy came home to find that 'boss had died'! The medical certification had confirmed that the man had actually died that early morning!

In my Columns and Books, I wrote about my late father who had Parkinson – and also hearing problems because of his age being over 88. My late father did not like wearing hearing aids – because he said it made him 'feel uncomfortable'! So it was difficult to communicate with him indeed! You had to shout and scream – and soon one by one 'gave up' on him!

The poor man – he used to see all people around him – children and grandchildren – having a field day – talking to each other in fun and merriment – whilst he sat on the chair – all alone – sad, desolate and unhappy! Few times I noticed sad tears coming from his eyes – especially when I sat near him – trying to talk to him – or at least not make him feel alone and miserable!

After all the sacrifices and things he did for his family! If you have read my books – especially The Between Us! Only Series – **www.myownmajid.com** – you will see so many stories about my late dad – Peace Be Upon Him! Also on my Late Mother – Peace Be Upon Her – Amin Amen for both! I have always heard the expression – what goes around – comes around! Maybe it is my turn now to experience what my late dad had experienced? Because I too made many sacrifices for my family! Same stories here at **www.myownmajid.com**

Like I had said before – it is not my intention to make mountains out of molehills – but I am a sick ailing man now – and even typing this makes me cry – remembering my late Father too! It also reminds me of my friend's advice – surrounded by so many people – but yet all alone too! I suffer from acute diabetes – I have eyes problems in glaucoma, myopia and eyes pressures!

I have noticed lately that I have developed a very bad temper and tantrums – because I am carrying too much excess baggage still with me! I still remember with bitterness and anger how my career life was 'screwed up' by me speaking my mind – and calling a spade as a spade! And how people worked together and conspired to bring my Management Consultancy down – by false promises, betrayals, double dealings and stab-in-the-backs! My websites, books and columns are full of these stories too!

The East Africans say also – The thing that bites you comes from your own dress! When the European Expatriates ran the show – things were not so bad – and until our very own came in – and they had long and elephant memories! Though the systems were in to 'practise freedom of speech' – they were not applied in full! People just hate my guts and me simply because I am not afraid to open my mouth and in speaking my mind!

And actual in not wanting things to go bad as my focus and aims in my life! That is my BIG PROBLEM – being honest, sincere, genuine – and forthcoming in life! My 2$^{nd}$ Arab Management book – A Cry For Help! – I wished those VIPs I had sent them Complimentary Copies had read it! My book website at **www.myown-majid.com** It was written BEFORE the Arab Spring Uprisings – and with all the cautionary calls, advices and counsels inside – as a Human Resources Management Consultant Expert and Advisor!

Yes on another thing! I am a Writer and Columnist too! I meet many who like what I write! But there are some elements – some powerful too – that wish for the dirt to be pushed under the carpet – or as some of them say – 'not to wash our dirty linen' in public! They too have a field day to make misery and havoc to me – even if the payments are peanuts – or there is simply no money in books! "Just do not support him!' syndromes! Especially from some expatriates even! As Jules Renard had said - *Writing is the only profession where no one considers you ridiculous if you earn no money!*

All my life I have been a quiet peaceful type of guy! I have always avoided confrontations – even if thrown at me! That is my second big problem – I try so much to avoid confrontation and fights – some people take this for me being weak, docile and impotent! That is not the real case – even if I will be speaking my mind – and in making a stand!

When I feel that the situation has crossed Red Lines – despite my earlier cautions, warnings and 'stay-away' – I come charging in – like a bull in a glassware shop! My 'negative reactions' – gives more chances and opportunities for those vicious and unscrupulous people – to use this more against me! That only enrages and makes me more mad – adding fuel to the fire! And the vicious cycle! And some people are always on a 'win win' situation – so they take more advantage, credit and benefit from this – whether by design, default or inadvertently.

I am now a 65 years old person – sick and ailing too! Bad mixtures, chemistry and abrasiveness just make me come out more worse! It brings out the worst in me – in the very things I desperately try to avoid and keep away. Some people are good Actors and Pretenders – and it is an uphill fight for me to remain at par!

I have always strived and aimed to be a nice, good and decent person – with care and feelings for everyone! I believe in Live and Let Live too – and one should not be too quick to judge – or condemn! And knowing the famous adage – *The one wearing the shoe knows where it most pinches!*

There are many other things I want to say here too – but cannot here because I do not want to hurt others – or shift blame and attention to them! Besides – this is a public forum!

**Take Care!**

**By: Majid Al-Suleimany**

# B.26        Life: A Rewind?

## For Wednesday September 25th 2013

- *We cannot reverse the past – but we can learn from it –* **WHO.**
- *Life is like a drama. You are given a role in it – and all you can do is cast your role well! –* **Miss Fernandes – My Literature Teacher**

**Sometime back, I was watching this English film** where there this woman who gets a vision dream of her  husband being killed in a nasty road accident - when a fuel truck explodes near her husband's 4-wheeler – and killing him instantly!

The film shows us in different scenarios   scenes where in one the wife is able to caution her husband not to go out at all – to one to not take the particular road – to one telling him to still go on the route - but still watch out for the oil truck - before it turns over and in its explosion involve him and his 4-wheeler! The beauty of the film is that it shows us what happens to the family in each scenario - with its rewind and forward of each one being played out it the film – and for your involvement to see what actually happens – in front of the scenes – and behind too!

Unfortunately, despite all the precautionary visionary mirage dream - the accident still happens – and the wife is shown as lamenting as to why she was not more forceful in stopping her husband not to venture out at all in the first place – and in the follow-up of making her husband realise of the awaiting dangers – even if the man had just sneeringly laughed it off – telling the wife she 'had seen too many films' - and is all but just fanciful imagination of her part and mind only!

Would not life be beautiful if you have reached a stalemate situation – or nearing a precipice disaster and calamity – to be able to pull back just in time? One of the Management theories is also called JIT – Just In Time. It is more related to Inventories and consequences in ROI – Return on Investments! This is in order to achieve continuous improvement key areas of focus could be flow, employee involvement and quality aspects.

Like also it entails – in the final analysis – of pulling off a particular unpleasant unwelcome corporate regulation or pursuit that may have overall more serious consequences and repercussions – if still instead were to go ahead and to put in practice! Also where in summary – you are also able to do just the right decisions and in time – before more mistakes and consequences ahead!

Life would be beautiful if we could foresee ahead on our planned actions and decisions – and see if we should go ahead or not? Or even if we had gone ahead – to be able to pull back just in time – before more serious consequences and repercussions!

In our faith we have a special prayer called **Istikhara** – means to seek goodness from Allah – and when one intends to do an important task! It is to seek guidance if the intended action is good for one or not? According to **Bukhari - Narrated Jabir bin 'Abdullah :The Prophet  - PBUH - used** to teach us the way of **doing Istikhara**, in all matters as he taught us the Suras of the Quran. He said, "If anyone of you thinks of doing any job (task) he should offer a two Rakat prayer and recite the following –

"O Allah! I seek goodness from Your Knowledge and with Your Power (and Might) I seek strength, and I ask from You Your Great Blessings, because You have the Power and I do not have the power. You Know everything and I do not know, and You have knowledge of the unseen. Oh Allah! If in Your Knowledge this action ---- ------------------------------------------- (which I intend to do) is better for my religion and faith, for my life and end [death], for here [in this world] and the hereafter then make it destined for me and make it easy for me and then add blessings [baraka'] in it, for me.

O Allah! In Your Knowledge if this action is bad for me, bad for my religion and faith, for my life and end [death], for here [in this world] and the hereafter then turn it away from me and turn me away from it and whatever is better for me, ordain [destine] that for me and then make me satisfied with it.

We need to go back to our Religion – and do things right and correct! The problems in the world now are that people are so much occupied with the material and consumerism world – and have left all ethics and values all behind! They just look at their own vested personal and selfish interests – what is in this for me if I do this? Or if I do not do this?

Then everyone is surprised and in shock - when things turn that bad and sour – and as usual we cover ourselves then – by shifting blame and responsibilities to others – find 'scapegoats' - as if we are the Angels brought to the face of the earth – and can do no wrong! Or harm! In actual fact – even butter does not melt on our mouth!

The irony of the world today is like Ali Baba and The Forty Thieves – name calling and saying to a 'petty thief' still on the learning curve – *Stop! You (unprintable) Nasty Thief!!*

**May Allah God Guide us all to the right path and ways – Amin Amen.**

**Take Care!**

**By: Majid Al-Suleimany - Date – September 13th 2013**

# C.01. The Omani Columnists!

## For Sunday September 29th 2013

- *I have given you good advice; but you like not good advisers* – Prophet Saleh RA 7:73 – 79
- *I am thankful for all those difficult people in my life; they have shown me exactly who I do not want to be* - Anon
- *If some of the Officials were to be at the Pearly Gates; simply no one will enter into heaven* – My Late Father

**This week I was very sad and disheartened in reading this column - in the other newspaper - of a famous Omani Lady Columnist from Salalah –** who had decided to stop continuing with her column. She does not give explicit and clear reasons for ending the column – but one can be forgiven by reading between the lines - that it was more of her decision to do so! I can associate with her feelings – having gone through the motions myself before!

This lady I admire her very much by being able to handle taboo subjects – especially from an angle of a woman – where in the conservativeness and inward looking at things – it is expected (required?) for the woman to go to a corner – and shut up! The poor ladies in another place are 'still not allowed to drive' – and if they do – their 'guardians' are charged hefty fines for allowing people under their control – to 'drive without licenses'!

Even though the young dynamic Emir of Qatar in his UN Speech had said - It is clear that things will not revert (to the old ways of doing things) in the Arab world and that the Arab peoples have now become more aware of their rights and are more involved in the public domain.

It is true that there are many people – including Omanis for that matter - that would prefer that there are no Omani Columnists that especially write in English – though I would imagine that there would be more time and compassion – for those that write in Arabic!

The problem is that in the many cases and in many of the English Newspapers especially here – you may find The Top Management being run by The Locals themselves – but the many of the Editorial and Media Staff are Expatriates! Trust me in saying that many of them they really do have more time, patience and support for the local writers – in many cases anyway! But there are still a group of the die-hards Old Guards that are determined to bring our lots down – and not even to be outdone.

With due respects and apologies – this is the sad and bitter truth. Even if some may deny and do not want to accept this! Woe to you if they are in control – or have 'the ears of the top (local) bosses' – and that they are very good Actors, Impersonators and Impressionists. Schemers and Plotters! They also have long elephant memories – and do not ever forget – or forgive easily. Once you have crossed them – you are doomed for life!

Even if Ghandi himself had said – *The weak can never forgive. Forgiveness is the attribute of the strong* - Mahatma Ghandi – Few of them listen to him.  Even Dr. Abdul Kalaam - *It is very easy to defeat someone, but it is very hard to win someone!* And Shakespeare too - *Never play with the feelings of others because you may win the game but the risk is that you will surely lose the person for a life time!*

**Bite the hand that feeds you – and then end to lick the boot that kicks you! – Anon**

**People need to realise that things have now changed** with the advent of time and development – and in Change! Change – before Changes change you! The old games and gimmicks do not work anymore. Personally, I do feel that those in The Senior Positions in The Media too need to change with The Times – and sitting back in the offices whilst the expatriates under them do all the works – and they then take credit and control – need to change too – and very fast too!

There is simply no time for 'foot dragging' – and in not in giving more chances and opportunities to the younger ones – especially those that have the Media qualifications and knowledge – even if not that much experience and exposures. Even The Expert Expatriate had made many mistakes – before he became now capable and competent. If the chances and breaks were given to them before – why not to our own too?

As a Writer and Columnist too - I have met many people who like what I write! But there are some elements – some powerful too – that wish for the dirt to be pushed under the carpet – or as some of them say to me – 'not to wash our dirty linen' in public! Especially as you write in English! Even if in writing the payments are just peanuts – or as it is said – that there is simply no money in writing! As Jules Renard had said - *Writing is the only profession where no one considers you ridiculous if you earn no money!*

For me personally, I am very happy to see so many youngsters coming up to in writing columns – especially in English! They should be encouraged and be supported! Like I had told The Editor – Anytime that you have found a good writer cum columnist – and have no space for more – just let me know to quit gracefully – whilst still being read and respected. One of The Young Columnist – whom I am seeing doing very well – has even called me The Guru – because of my support to him in the past!

We need to be more open and flexible – and more receptive! We owe this to the younger generation – to our future, destiny and legacy. History will judge us unkindly and mercilessly - if we do not come to do of that is required and expected for to do and perform! Time is of the essence too! No time to waste here!

**And Yes – Those like us that still like to 'open our mouth and speak'? Let us! You never know! One day we may have nothing more to say! Or may have said it already!**

**Take Care!**

**By: Majid Al-Suleimany**

**Date – September 13<sup>th</sup> 2013**

## C.02        Drink and Fly?

### Or The Mixing of Drinks and Drugs - Whilst Flying!

### For Wednesday October 2nd 2013

**We always talk of DUI - Driving Under The Influence? But Drink and Fly too?**

**I was reading this scary news of some pilots admitting** that they had gone to sleep whilst flying - in some cases both pilots at the same time! If that is not scary enough - I do not know what is! Unless one of them has 'fake licenses' in flying! As a kid - one of my life's ambitions was to be a Pilot. Indeed, I believe that I would have made a good one too - if the qualifications were more directed 'at not smoking and drinking at all' - amongst the others!

**I was really intrigued to watch this film** *Flight* - it is a 2012 American drama film starring Denzel Washington (Whip Whitaker) - and was nominated for the Academy Awards. The film message and theme is the 'destruction of the family home' by being Alcoholic - usually by the man - but in some cases for both the couple - in a worst case scenario! The victims - in any case - are the children more - if they too do not develop to being 'alcoholics and drugs victims' - and even prostitution - because of broken homes! In many cases, the vicious cycle continuous with them not being able to be 'good parents' to their children too!

**About The Film.** On October 14, 2011, Airline captain Whip Whitaker - Denzel Washington -) awakens in his Orlando hotel room with flight attendant Katerina Márquez - Nadine Velazquez -) after a night of sex, drinking, drug use, and very little sleep. After using cocaine to wake up, he boards SouthJet Flight 227 as pilot to Atlanta. After Whip threads the plane through severe turbulence at takeoff, copilot Ken Evans takes over while Whip discreetly mixes vodka in his orange juice and takes a nap.

He is jolted awake as the plane begins its descent, and the aircraft goes into a steep dive. Unable to regain pitch control, Whip rolls the plane upside down to arrest the dive. While this is happening in the cockpit a young boy hasn't done his seat belt properly so Katerina undoes her seat belt saving the child but ultimately causing her death.

Meanwhile Nicole - Kelly Reilly -) is seen going out of her house to her drug dealer after begging for some heroin she is giving some, but an extremely strong dosage and is told only to smoke it and some cocaine for if she gets depressed. When she returns home she finds her door unlocked and enters to find her landlord. She tricks him and locks him out before knocking over her box of drugs seeing the needle she insert the heroin and injects herself before having an overdose. As she is wheeled out of the house by a paramedic the upside down plane is seen flying over the flats.

Back on the plane with the engines failing he realizes they will not make it to a runway, so he rolls the plane upright and manages to make a forced landing in a field. He loses consciousness on impact and is dragged out of the aircraft by a passenger.Whip awakens in an Atlanta hospital with minor injuries, where he is greeted by his old friend Charlie Anderson - Bruce Greenwood -), who represents the airline's Pilots Union.

He tells Whip that he saved 96 out of 102 people on board, 2 crew and 4 passengers, but an National Transportation Safety Board (NTSB) official informs him Katerina was among those killed. While sneaking a cigarette in the stairwell, Whip meets Nicole, who is recovering from an overdose of heroin, and promises to visit her when they leave the hospital. In the morning, his friend and drug dealer, Harling Mays John Goodman -), picks him up and sneaks him away from the hospital.

Whip drives to his late father's farm and dumps out all his alcohol. When he meets Charlie and attorney Hugh Lang - Don Cheadle -), they explain that the NTSB performed a toxicology screen while he was unconscious, showing that Whip was intoxicated. The results could send him to prison on alcohol, drug, and manslaughter charges. Hugh promises to get the toxicology report voided on technical grounds, but Whip leaves in a fury and seeks out Nicole.

He finds her bailing on her lease, bribes her landlord not to pursue her, and brings her to the farm. Nicole and Whip soon become intimate, but Whip begins drinking again while Nicole is trying to stay clean and sober. He then attends Katerina Márquez funeral whereupon he meets Margaret he persuades her to tell the NTSB that he was sober upon the day of the crash.

Nicole brings him to a recovery meeting. Whip leaves early to visit with his Co-pilot Ken Evans who remains hospitalized, has recently come out of his induced coma, but remains severely injured. He tells Whip that both his legs and pelvis are crushed and his has little to no chance of walking unaided and no chance of ever flying a plane again.

Whip is sympathetic towards Evans injuries. However Evans explains how he knew Whip was drunk and how he could smell the gin and vodka on Whip, but believes all people where put on earth for a reason and Whips hasn't come yet. So therefore Evans will not tell the NSTB about Whip being drunk.

Nicole and Whip catch up with each other back at the farm. Whip importunes Nicole to run away with him. She demurs: and as soon as Whip is drunk again, Nicole leaves.

When Whip finds the media outside his farm's gate, he drives drunk to the home of his ex-wife and son, who compel him to leave. In leaving his wife's home, he is mobbed by the press and clearly presents as not playing with a full deck. Whip flees to Charlie's home and begs to stay with Charlie's family, vowing not to drink again before the NTSB hearing. The night before the hearing, Whip is moved into a guarded hotel room to ensure he does not get drunk. His minibar has only nonalcoholic beverages, but when he finds the door to the adjacent room unlocked, Whip discovers it has a full minibar.

Charlie and Hugh find him the next morning, passed out, and still intoxicated. They call Harling, who revives him with cocaine for the hearing. At the hearing, Ellen Block - Melissa Leo - the lead NTSB investigator, explains that a damaged elevator assembly jackscrew was the primary cause of the crash. She commends Whip on his valor and skill, explaining that no other pilots were able to land the plane in simulations following the crash.

Then she reveals that two empty vodka bottles were found in the trash of the plane, but none were served to the passengers. Only one of the crew's toxicology reports was positive for alcohol, although one was excluded. Since Katerina's report was positive for alcohol, Block asks Whip if he believes that she drank it. Rather than lie and permanently taint her good name, Whip admits that he drank it, that he flew intoxicated, and that he is intoxicated at that moment.

Thirteen months later, an imprisoned Whip tells a support group of fellow inmates that he is glad to be sober and does not regret doing the right thing, because he finally feels "free". He tells the support group he lost his piloting license, but not his faith in telling the truth.

He has pictures of Nicole and other family and friends on the wall of his cell, along with greeting cards congratulating him on being sober for a year. He is working to rebuild his relationship with his son, who visits his father to talk with him about a college application essay on "the most fascinating person I've never met." His son begins by asking, "Who are you?" Whip replies "That's a good question."

**Take Care!**

**By: Majid Al-Suleimany**

**Date – September 30th 2013**

**Words – 1022**

**www.majidall.com – www.majidwrite.com – www.myownmajid.com**

# C.03          System Overload!

### Or Just The Lack of Job Responsibilities, Ethics and Professionalism!

## For Sunday October 6th 2013

- *O you who believe! Fear Allah and be with the true ones (in word and deed)* - **The Holy Quran - 9:119**
- *Life cannot defeat a Writer who is in love with writing, for life itself is a Writer's love until death* - **Edna Ferber**
- *It is a wastage of energy to be angry with a man who behaves badly, just as it is to be angry with a car that won't go* - **Bertrand Russell**

**System Overload** - According to Mosby's Medical Dictionary - *System Overload* is an inability to cope with messages and expectations from a number of sources within a given time limit. Not to be confused with also **"System Overload"** - which is a garage rock song by New Zealand Rock and Roll band The Datsuns. It is their second single off the album Smoke & Mirrors. It was released on both Vinyl and Compact Disk in 2006. It is typical of The Datsuns style. With loud guitar, a lead break and dominant vocals. Electricians describe it when 'electricity 'trips down' (shuts down!)!

With the very start of this column over 12 years ago - I had resolved to speak the truth - even if it will cost me! And cost me it did - but that has not deterred me! My first article was titled More Dangerous and Troubled Waters Ahead! And everything that I had said in it - and others that followed - all came out in truth and in reality!

Mark Twain had said - *Always do right. This will gratify some people and astonish the rest!* Also in our Hadith - *If one of you sees something wrong, let him change it with his own hand; if he cannot, then raise voice and speak out against it; if he cannot do even that, then dislike or hate it in your heart, but that is the lowest degree of faith!* And on Truth - *Say what is true, although it may be bitter and displeasing to people!* - By Baihaqi.

The other day I had gone to this Electronic shop to buy a new laptop after my current one went obsolete. There were three Sales People - all expatriates - attending to one European Expatriate. So I sidled to the one salesman on the outer and asked him about the models that I was interested and within my limited budget. Just like I would like to drive the Top Model Range Rover - but I have to consent to staying with my 8 year old banger Camry - because I cannot get the Hire Purchase to buy a new one - even if I can afford it - because of my age. You see I am over 55 - and already put in the list of the 'living dead' here! That is how life is now - and how the cookie crumbles!

Anyway, the more friendlier of the lot - guess it was a Filipino - pointed to the direction of where I could see the machines that I was interested in! Maybe he saw me intently looking at the machines - or maybe he thought I would steal or spoil something - then he reluctantly came over! As I had done my research already - I told him to reduce the price - because I needed an up to date Printer also! The good man did!

As I was going out - this nice European lady - from the goodness of her heart - turned to the Salesmen reprimanding them - *See you all ignored him - and he bought these things from you! Yet all of you were concentrating with us - ignoring him - and all we are doing here is 'window shopping'! Let that be a lesson for you in the future!* That cooled me down greatly from the 'milk of humane kindness' - and made me feel so bad for a considerable while after that!

And this is the point I want to make here! Maybe there are a few bad eggs or fish in the basket - but the trend and approach is 'controlled apathy and disdain' against the locals - for no other reason than dislike and ridicule - and contempt! They try hard to hide it - but if you have even an iota of perception - you will not fail to notice it! Especially nowadays! I do not why these things are happening to us locals now? Maybe we are all made to blame to what is happening to some of them - so the whole lot of us have to be penalised and to be punished in turn!

This is not only in shops - but in the Offices too - including the so-called high profile places - and more even by the locals to their fellow locals - and especially in situations where the expatriates still dominate and control - and the top locals are just window dressings - or 'figure heads' only! With all the works and initiatives still being done by the expatriates - and who are ready and willing for the local boss to take points and credit - even if they (expatriates) remain not in the limelight and exposure!

Woe to you if you antagonise the Mafia lots - and a few of them have 'the ears' of the local bosses. The Local bosses are good Actors, Performers and Impersonators - and if you go to complain and grudge - they pretend to be attentive and caring - whilst all the time working against you! I know I am talking of few misguided cases - but their damages are more harmful and devastating - especially if they come from the so-called high profile places! Red lines have been crossed so many times before - but people just do not care - and still keep pushing!

I do not know how long these things will go on - before there is an explosion - like that cinder fire burning underneath and within heatedly and unseen - until it just surfaces - intently and heatedly! I have said so many times in this column - Do not bite the hand that feeds you - because you may end licking the boot that kicks you! They also say - *Those that do not learn from history - are apt to repeat the mistakes of the past!*

**Take Care!**

**By: Majid Al-Suleimany**

**Date – September 30th 2013**

## C.04          The Basic Necessities of Life!
### For Wednesday October 9th 2013

The description of Necessities in the Dictionary -   Supplies, Provisions, Requirements, Food etc. The meaning of Necessities also encompasses the following:-

- Something necessary or indispensable: *food, shelter, and other necessities of life.*

- The fact of being necessary or indispensable; indispensability: *the necessity of adequate housing.*

- An imperative requirement or need for something: *the necessity for a quick decision..*

- The state or fact of being necessary or inevitable: *to face the necessity of testifying in court.*

- An unavoidable need or compulsion to do something: *not by choice but by necessity.*

**In the Jungle Book Cartoon Film - Mowgli The Bear sings - The Bare Necessities**

Look for the bare necessities - The simple bare necessities - Forget about your worries and your strife - I mean the bare necessities - Old Mother Nature's recipes - That brings the bare necessities of life

Wherever I wander, wherever I roam - I couldn't be fonder of my big home - The bees are buzzing in the tree - To make some honey just for me - When you look under the rocks and plants - And take a glance at the fancy ants - Then maybe try a few

**Chorus** - The bare necessities of life will come to you - They'll come to you!

Look for the bare necessities - The simple bare necessities - Forget about your worries and your strife - I mean the bare necessities - That's why a bear can rest at ease -

With just the bare necessities of life

Now when you pick a pawpaw - Or a prickly pear - And you prick a raw paw - Next time beware - Don't pick the prickly pear by the paw - When you pick a pear - Try to use the claw - But you don't need to use the claw - When you pick a pear of the big pawpaw - Have I given you a clue ?

**Chorus** - The bare necessities of life will come to you - They'll come to you!

So just try and relax, yeah cool it - Fall apart in my backyard - 'Cause let me tell you something little britches - If you act like that bee acts, uh uh -You're working too hard

And don't spend your time looking around - For something you want that can't be found - When you find out you can live without it - And go along not thinking about it

I'll tell you something true - The bare necessities of life will come to you!

I am not sure who said it - but it could be Pervez ex Pakistan Leader or Mahathir Mohamed - ex Malaysian Leader - who said that people are only more interested in life in The Basic Necessities of Life like Air, Food, Water, Shelter and Clothing - though some would also add Health and Love to the equation. People are lesser interested in higher buildings, bigger roads and flyovers, bigger airports and seaport - or newer industries and projects - or schemes. That is for them to live and survive the Basic Necessities of Life are more paramount and predominant!

Al Jazeera Television was showing these families that had lost loved ones in the sinking boats refugees cases - and why they travelled in these perilous and dangerous trips to look for life and shelter in Europe, Australia etc.

They replied they were already the 'dead living' in their own countries and 'dying slowly' due to the internal strife in their own countries with constant bombings, killings and kidnappings - drugs, alcoholism and prostitution - and with no jobs or futures even!

They simply had to make the trips in trying 'for better life and future' elsewhere - taking on board all their families - including children and even babies too! Despite all these tragedies - people are still trying to go overseas - and have just not given up in trying!

I was watching this live candid documentary by Al Jazeera Television about life in Libya post the Arab Springs - titled - *The Road to Tawergha.* - As Libya emerges from the shadows of dictatorship, it must decide whether to embrace retribution or reconciliation - In 2011, Libyans rose up against their leader, Muammar Gaddafi, as the Arab Spring took root in the north African country . The Tawerghans are a distinct ethnic racial (black skinned) minority - who are made to suffer now a lot of unfairness and injustices as a result of their supposed support to the Ghaddafi regime

They are now IDPs - Internal Displaced People (Persons) - and seeing this film documentary - you get 'live vivid pictures and examples' of what are the basic necessities of life. A group of children are seen singing in the end - that they want to go back to their abandoned homes for safety and in peace- and are not really interested in 'macaroni and pasta' etc - but to be back home and free - as others too in the country. Much of the town's almost 30,000-strong population fled. Some sought sanctuary in Benghazi in the east; others in Tripoli in the west and Sabha in the south. Most of the refugees are black skinned Libyans.

The film has pointed and distinct homing  theme of that regime that was able to incite hatred between the Libyans peoples. With the new Libyan government so far failing to embrace the notion of national reconciliation - some Libyans are taking it upon themselves to pursue peace and forgiveness.  And demonstrated in the film of the South African example in Reconciliation - and not in Retribution!

*The Road to Tawergha* is about war, retribution and the difficult road to reconciliation that Libya must travel if it is to emerge from the shadows of Gaddafi's 42-year reign. It is also about the Basic Necessities of Life - and how far people can be pushed in its pursuits!

**Real revealing and an Eye Opener! Take Care!**

**By: Majid Al-Suleimany**

**Date – September 30th 2013**

## C.05        Being Exemplary In Life!
### For Sunday October 12th 2013

- *Be a first rate version of yourself, not a second rate version of someone else* - **Judy Garland**
- *Be the change that you want to see in the world!*- **Mahatma Gandhi**

We constantly hear these phrases being said - Act your position! Act your role! Be yourself! Please be professional - ethical - principled! We expect better things from you - not you doing this instead! Maybe people are too long in jobs - and they have come to feel indispensable - or nothing can touch them now! Or nobody cares - so why should I?

Or yet still - with due respects - but ...! Or - I am sorry (not my role) to say this to you - but I think...! Or he is the best example of what a Manager (CEO) should be! Or a Human Resources, Finance, Media, Engineer etc. professional should be! Or a True Leader - he leads by examples and deeds! Or the other side of the coin - Act your position! Act your level! Act your standing! Be your real self - person!

What if a parent or teacher does not behave and act for one? In the Western world - your own children can be taken away from you - and be put in Social Care and Adoption - if you do not behave like parents are required to behave, act and perform - and when you are in danger to your own children!

What if a Human Resources HR Professional does not behave, act and perform as one? If you who is supposed to be 'The Conscience Keeper' of the establishment - and even more than the CEO or Director? It is not only representing the Management - going by the books - and the easy way of doing things - and ignoring the employees - who look upon you to sort their issues too - even if in confrontation and in disputes with Management?

That is what makes the mantle of true HR - and what shines out - or not? To be able to confront Management - when they are in the wrong - or have made or going to make mistakes - and gross errors in thinking and in judgment! I can tell you - HR is not an easy job - it is not only Admin - and doing visas renewals!

What if you are in Finance and or in Audits? And you see wrong practices being made - not only in operations - but fraud, bribery and corruption? But you go along - because you are afraid more of 'keeping your job' - and being on 'the protective nice side of yourself' - why should I care - so long as I get my pay? Trust me - when heads will roll - yours will too without escape?

And what if you are in The Media? Or as an Engineer? Or in the other professions? Where you are required to act your role and position - and be the example to follow

- lead by examples - and not you joining the league in bad, wrong, unprofessional, unprincipled and unethical practices?

As a young boy - I used to hear especially my father lament - you are the eldest (Mother side) - and you are supposed to set an example to be copied - and not you as the eldest to fight with your brothers - and worse with your sisters! My late father used to say to me - you hold the responsibilities of being the eldest. It is a heavy responsibility! Act your age! Act your role! Or you just wastage of space and air! Eldest - but not worth the label! In my crooked ways of thinking, sometimes I used to think that my parents did not just like me!

We have seen these films like Whistle Blower - where the heroine stands to lose everything - including her own life even - by exposing great institutions like UN for 'covering up' human trafficking in ex war torn areas of the world - where even the top guys want to 'push the dirt under the carpet'?

There are now many institutions where 'Whistle Blowers' are encouraged, defended and protected - under new 'Good Governance' practices and principles. Not even in companies and state institutions, NGOs etc. - but even to higher levels - like even Presidents like Nixon were exposed in the great Watergate scandals. Remember the Frost interview?

When I had started working in that distant land - I saw live examples of malpractices of creating 'artificial shortages' of certain high brands fuel - and the disease and malaise went even to the highest echelon levels. When the exposure came out - yours truly Mr. Clean - was asked to run the affairs in Marketing and Operations - after the exposure!

I remember telling the Top Regional guy of the trends - and he fooled me by saying to me - Thanks for telling us! Keep us informed - the subject material of even good Thriller Films! I came to know far later - after the exposure! The East Africans have an expression - you can steal for 39 days - on the 40th you will be exposed!

In my Consultancy career jobs I have met many fellow locals that took 'great pleasure and enjoyment' in delaying my due payments - even after delivery and continuous extra works and requirements! Some even stretching to more than 5 to 6 months - yet they are regular - and even pay three fold the rate to the International ones? Some even have denied to pay me - under flimsy and minor technicalities!

Yet still this same week we suffered a lot of water problems in Qorum Heights! Even the hotlines - the emergencies line - nobody even answered! Why should we? We have already told some of them - why bother to repeat? Let them suffer! And so many other things too! How long will these things go on - before there is breaking point? What is really happening to us now? I just dread to hear the answer! Don't you?

# APPENDICES

# A    The Arab Manager: The Call!

## About The Book!

## www.createspace.com/5083875

**This is a book re-do of my previous book – Original Book - A Cry For Help!** It was suggested to me by an American CEO friend of mine who had read all my books – including the Arab Management ones! He commented that though this particular book was very important – it did not take off well in reading and reception like the Psychology book which had won The USA Gold Seal Literary Excellence for 2013 (Eric Hoffer)! The reasons were plain people misjudging the book by a cover of a Crying Lady who was not even Arab – and the first chapter being dominated as being traumatized at the time of the death of my Mother!

With changes in removing some of those chapters (and images!) of The Arab Office Environment showing radicalization, extremism and fundamentalism of The Society as most of the events are now past in references with the current status in The Middle East Post The Arab Spring Uprisings!

Though the original book had acted as an Omen and Predictor of events that came to realization post the book publication in 2009. It was my earnest prayer and wish that people – especially in The Leadership – to have read this book! Anyway, I am not the person that likes to say – again and again – I told you so!

I have decided also not to add many images than necessary to expedite the book coming out together with the new book – Arab Management: Reality or Myth? The Arab Manager! www.createspace.com/4960056 and previous book - Psychology of Arab Management Thinking! – www.trafford.com/08-0889

This book, therefore, will be the 4th book in Arab Management Series and my 18th book to date – 3 books are also in Road Safety – and the rest assorted from my Columns and Writings. 2 of the books are about Reviews and Accolades received on all my books to date!

My Columns, Writings etc. are here at www.majidwrite.com and www.majidall.com

Also, another important and pertinent remark to make here is that this book was being published at the time of death of my late Mother PBUH and was so emotionalized and traumatized to make her article - I wrote for her – titled Goodbye; Our Mama! In Memoriam! Thus Readers may have felt the book was more 'of a novel' rather than serious stuff in Arab Management lapses, shortcomings etc.

For the same reason few images will be added to this book also.

I hope those who had misread the original Book Cover of a Crying Lady! And the aforementioned will now read this book having clarified and in transparency all the aforementioned.

Suffice also to say that despite 6 years later things at the work front – its surroundings and atmosphere has just gone more bad and stale – on the verge of the precipice, decadence, malaise and associated – just like that cinder fire burning intensely underground before it erupts.

For this status quo, I recommend that you read this book with my new Arab Book as aforementioned.

**Wish me (us!) luck! - Majid Al Suleimany**

# B    ARAB MANAGEMENT BOOKS (PREVIOUS)

### The Arab Management Books

www.myownmajid.com - www.myown-ebooks.com

www.bethesafedriver.com

## C.00        Books on Road Safety!

## By Majid Al Suleimany

### September 1, 2014

### Arabic – Behind The Wheel!

## About The Book!

خلف عجلة القيادة

أن تكون سائقًا آمِنًا

ماجد السليماني

www.createspace.com/4875352

www.bethesafedriver.com - www.myownmajid.com
www.myown-ebooks.com

- **أُخِذت بقراءة الكتاب، حتى إنني أعدت التفكير في ما اعتقدت أني كنت أعرفه عن السلامة على الطريق. رئيس تنفيذي لشركة بريطانية**
- **تأثَّرت كثيرًا بما ورد من قصص مأساوية مرعبة في الكتاب. مدير عام عماني**

تشير الإحصائيات إلى أن سلطنة عمان من بين البلدان التي تشهد أعلى عدد من الحوادث المرورية والإصابات الناجمة عنها على مستوى العالم. ومع انتشار السلوكيات المتهورة في قيادة السيارات فإنه من الأهمية بمكان البدء في تغيير الثقافة السائدة في استخدام الطرق. يقدم هذا الكتاب الجديد والرائد البراهين الدالَّة على أهمية الالتزام قواعد السلامة أثناء قيادة المركبة.

يحفل الكتاب بالعديد من القصص المؤلمة والمؤثرة مُبيِّنًا مخاطر الطريق والثمن الباهظ الذي يدفعه السائق جرَّاء تقصيره. ومع تأكيد كبار المسؤولين على أهمية السلامة على الطريق، آن الأوان ليكون سائقو المركبات أكثر حذرًا في القيادة. إن هذا الكتاب القيَّم؛ "أن تكون سائقًا آمنًا! خلف عجلة القيادة! سرد جديد عن السلامة على الطريق" من شأنه أن ينقذ حياة الكثيرين في أنحاء البلاد.

يفتح هذا الكتاب أعيننا على أهمية السلامة على الطريق والقيادة الآمنة، وذلك من خلال مجموعة من القصص الواقعية يسردها ضحايا الحوادث المرورية الذين يرغبون بنقل تجاربهم للآخرين ومشاركتهم الدروس والعبر لتثقيف سائقي السيارات في كل مكان في الوطن. يجدر بكل من يمسك بعجلة القيادة أن يقرأ هذا الكتاب الذي لا يُقدَّر بثمن ويمكنه أن ينقذ الكثيرين.

مستلهمًا الحادث المروّع الذي ألمَّ بعائلة زميل لنا في العمل يسعى الكتاب إلى تشجيع القيادة الآمنة حول العالم. ويأمل الكتاب من خلال سرد قصص الحوادث المرورية والخسائر الناجمة عنها أن يلقى صداه لدى القُرَّاء. إن القيادة المتهورة دائمًا لها عواقبها سواء نتجت عن الحادث إصابات أو خسائر في الأرواح أو الممتلكات أو حتى صدمات نفسية. يمنح هذا الكتاب قُرَّاءه الأسباب المقنعة ليكونوا سائقين آمنين.

يُشاد بهذا الكتاب باعتباره من أهم الكتب التي صدرت هذا العام، ويُتوقَّع أن يكون له تأثير كبير.

سيكون هذا الكتاب هو الكتاب الذي تنتظره الدولة ويباركه أهم الشخصيات في المجتمع بدءًا من حضرة صاحب الجلالة السلطان قابوس بن سعيد المعظم، حفظه الله ورعاه، إلى سماحة الشيخ أحمد بن حمد الخليلي، المفتي العام للسلطنة. وبأهدافه النبيلة وطرقه الفعَّالة يهدف هذا الكتاب إلى إحداث نقلة نوعية في حياة كل سائق.

**نص الغلاف الخلفي**

تشير الإحصائيات إلى أن سلطنة عمان من بين البلدان التي تشهد أعلى عدد من الحوادث المرورية والإصابات الناجمة عنها على مستوى العالم. ومع انتشار السلوكيات المتهورة في قيادة السيارات فإنه من الأهمية بمكان البدء في تغيير الثقافة السائدة في استخدام الطرق. يقدم هذا الكتاب الجديد والرائد البراهين الدالة على أهمية الالتزام قواعد السلامة أثناء قيادة المركبة.

يحفل الكتاب بالعديد من القصص المؤلمة والمؤثرة مُبيّنًا مخاطر الطريق والثمن الباهظ الذي يدفعه السائق جرّاء تقصيره. ومع تأكيد كبار المسؤولين على أهمية السلامة على الطريق، آن الأوان ليكون سائقو المركبات أكثر حذرًا في القيادة. إن هذا الكتاب القيّم؛ "أن تكون سائقًا آمنًا! خلف عجلة القيادة! سرد جديد عن السلامة على الطريق" من شأنه أن ينقذ حياة الكثيرين في أنحاء البلاد.

يفتح هذا الكتاب أعيننا على أهمية السلامة على الطريق والقيادة الآمنة، وذلك من خلال مجموعة من القصص الواقعية يسردها ضحايا الحوادث المرورية الذين يرغبون بنقل تجاربهم للآخرين ومشاركتهم الدروس والعبر لتثقيف سائقي السيارات في كل مكان في الوطن. يجدر بكل من يمسك بعجلة القيادة أن يقرأ هذا الكتاب الذي لا يُقدَّر بثمن ويمكنه أن ينقذ الكثيرين.

مستلهمًا الحادث المروّع الذي ألمّ بعائلة زميل لنا في العمل يسعى الكتاب إلى تشجيع القيادة الآمنة حول العالم. ويأمل الكتاب من خلال سرد قصص الحوادث المرورية والخسائر الناجمة عنها أن يلقى صداه لدى القُرّاء. إن القيادة المتهورة دائمًا لها عواقبها سواء نتجت عن الحادث إصابات أو خسائر في الأرواح أو الممتلكات أو حتى صدمات نفسية. يمنح هذا الكتاب قُرّاءه الأسباب المقنعة ليكونوا سائقين آمنين.

**الكتاب ـ هل كلّه عن قيادة السيارات!**

يقوم الكتاب على قصص واقعية حول الحوادث المرورية وضحاياها؛ وأثرها على حياتهم وحياة عائلاتهم من حولهم، والعبر والدروس التي يتعلّمها الآخرون من هذه القصص.

لو أن حادثًا مروريًا واحدًا أمكن تجنّبه بقراءة هذا الكتاب، فإن المقصد منه سيتحقّق!

\*\*\*

# خلف عجلة القيادة

### أن تكون سائقًا آمنًا

## ماجد السليماني

# Arabic – Behind The Wheel!
# Being The Safe Driver!

## By Majid Al Suleimany

- Gripping read that made me rethink what I thought I knew on Road Safety Awareness! – **British CEO**

- Touched my heart with such rending tragic horrifying stories! – **Omani GM**

The Sultanate of Oman has one of the highest numbers of automobile accidents and casualties in the world. With such rampant and reckless automobile behaviors on the rise, there has never been a better time to change the culture and safety of our roads. With this groundbreaking new book, drivers across the nation will finally have proof in hand as to why they should drive safer.

Filled with heartbreaking and emotional true stories, this illuminating book shows drivers everywhere the dangers of the road and the true cost of negligence. With high-ranking officials across the country acknowledging the importance of road safety, it is time for drivers everywhere to be more careful and drive safer. An invaluable road safety tool! *Behind the Wheel, Being the Safe Driver! New Road Safety Book* can save lives all across the country.

This eye-opening book emphasizes the importance of road safety and careful driving through a collection of real-life stories from accident victims who share the hard experiences and lessons they learned in order to better educate drivers everywhere. A vital read for anyone behind the wheel, this priceless book has the ability to save lives!

Inspired by a horrific crash which took the lives of a coworker's family - *Being the Safe Driver! Behind The Wheel!* - strives to encourage safer driving across the world. Filled with dramatic, true stories of accidents and loss, the book's poignant moments are sure to resonate with all readers.
Whether an accident results in injury, property loss, or simply a shaken emotional self, reckless driving always has consequences. From horrible injuries to destroyed families, this enlightening book does a fantastic job of giving all readers reasons to become safe drivers.

# For Direct Ordering!

**Behind The Wheel!**  www.createspace.com/4655681

**Being The Safe Driver!** www.createspace.com/4097374

**List of Contents – Pages - 41 - 44**

**D.00        Arab Management: Reality or Myth?**

## The Arab Manager!

## Arab Management: Reality or Myth?

## The Arab Manager!

www.createspace.com/4960056

### Why I Wrote This Book!

- *Do not tell me you are going to write this book! I just cannot believe it! –* **British CEO**
- *I thought after your last book – and the end of your columns – you will stop writing! You have me pleasantly surprised! –* **Senior Omani Public Official (Retired)**

This is my Third Arab Management Book after *Psychology of Arab*

***Management Thinking!*** And ***A Cry For Help!*** **And my 12th book! Three books are on Road Safety and the balance are based on my columns and writings!**

The book focuses on what is particular about the type of local Arab Management, its context and perspectives, and what is peculiar, special, or particular to that work in the context and in comparison to the Management Styles of other nations. Using personal experiences, examples, and illustrations, Al Suleimany exposes the new reality and truth and moves away from the trend and approach of hiding issues and problems. The books are soul searching, in deep self-analysis and critical evaluation of one's own people in the field.

The Author extols the culture and importance of work in his religion and the pitfalls and lackluster attitude of some of the Managers in position about the Accountabilities, Principles, Transparencies, Professionalism and Ethics of Management – and vis-à-vis their roles, aspects and responsibilities.

The Arab countries are far richer with abundant reserves and more importantly with a healthy and young population. In spite of all these why do we lag behind others in many spheres? Is there anything wrong with the Arab Management? He says, "He is baffled and confused".

"As Arabs, work is worshipped as if it is in praying. Arabs are also brought up to be polite, courteous and decent (at least a majority of us). Abrupt, ugly, rudeness and distort are discouraged. Also it is not easy to say NO – as part of the culture, customs, traditions and heritage. So what went wrong here – especially in management circles? Why are we behind the rest of the world, despite all our riches and resources?"

The Gulf Cooperation Council countries are some of the richest ones in the world. Despite the Middle East holding huge gas and oil reserves of the world, very little is known about the area, in particular about Arabian Management aspects.

All my Arab Management books have been written after a major upheaval in my life at the work front and elsewhere involving my life! I was always under the impression that my book A Cry For Help! was going to be my last book in Arab Management with the events that followed proving my case why 'I needed help!' as an Arab Manager! Though trying best to keep to myself – and trying to avoid conflict and confrontations as much as I possibly could – but people would not leave me alone! They were still after me!

I then decided to accept the challenge and write this book. Like the other books – I have tried to be as factual as possible – and with my usual style of writing of speaking to you directly from my heart – and to be as sincere, genuine, frank, forthright as possible – so that this book can not only be used in Research works – but as a Guide and Beacon for the children, grandchildren, great grandchildren – and future generations.

It is my Final Attempt to highlight a 'Quickly Deteriorating Situation' before malaise, stalemate and decadence sets in at The Work Front and its environment! In this book nobody has been spared – and that includes even myself too as The Author!

**Majid Al Suleimany**

**The Author - November 11, 2014**

# E        The Final Touch Down!

## End of My Columns!

- Great Works, Dear Majid! Please keep up the good works! – Dr. Faris Al Hajri
- Congratulations and Well Done! – Dr. Najma Al Zidjali (SQU)
- Pleased to see the positive reactions and impacts of your books – Raoul Restucci (MD PDO)
- Your book is a great beacon for now and the coming generations – Mohamed Anwar Al Balushi

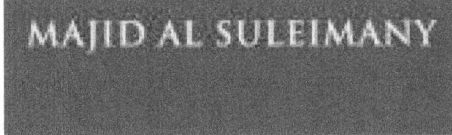

www.createspace.com/5058112

### About The Book!

**This is my 8th book in The Between Us Only! Series and my 15th book to date!** In this book, I have included the articles that came out after the above. Including my some 'touching feeling articles' to fill in the book – as there were only a handful of articles then that were out of my books!

Probably my last book - I hope you will enjoy reading my books – especially with The Between Us Only! Series as the columns have now 'naturally died' and ended as most things in life one day do!

It was a very difficult time to write especially this book and see The End of My Columns! But as they say – Do not cry because it has ended – but be happy because it has happened!

It was more of a hobby, self-satisfying and self-gratification in my writings and was never intended to make money! There is no money in books – as I found out the hard way – and as they say – **Writing is the only profession that no one considers you ridiculous if you make no money!** – Jules Renard.

***

I should know because Reading Habits are scarce and rare in our part of the world with especially now things like Facebook, WhatsUp, Instagram, LinkedIn etc. I was also advised to translate my Road Safety Books – **www.createspace.com/4655681** - Behind The Wheel! And to sell it at dismal price of about 12 Dollars only (Omani Rials 5) – but the boxes of books remain unsold at home from 'expected hopes in sales'…in actual fact people still want signed copies but as Free Complimentary Gifts – that is how cheap people have become.

Frankly - and smugly put - There is simply No Support for Omani Writers, Authors and Columnists – and Artists – apart from The Usual Hyperbole and Rhetoric – only for Images and Media purposes only!

**What more can I say now? Take Care and Bye!**

**Majid Said Nasser Al Suleimany**

**November 11, 2014**

***

**F.00          Between Us Only! The Original! (Redo!)**

**A Sense of Déjà vu! Between Us Only! From The Original!**
**www.createspace.com/5060552**

**Between Us Only! The Original! From The Original Book!**
**www.createspace.com/5041985**

**Twin Copies.**

**The original book was published on around May 2003 in Oman by Al Nahda Printing Press.**

Surprisingly, despite my 12 books later - there is still a large following who still think that this was my Best Book! I would not know – but surely it was My First Book! Compiling all my articles in my columns then Between Us Only! And At My Workplace in The Oman Daily Observer!

You can still find this book still in many offices in Oman – and that is really touching to me as The Author! The other day my brother in law MYS was 'scolding me' that I should have translated this book into Arabic – instead of the book Arabic – Behind The Wheel! – **www.createspace.com/4875352** He is one of my most advertent Reader and fan!

As there are only few copies left circulating around, I thought it fit to preserve the works by redoing the book! I was debating to add pictures and images – and to sort out by topics – but in the end decided to try as best as to add some images in! The aforementioned were 'the usual pointers and complaints' mainly raised on the book. The first book was sponsored by The MB Group of Companies and carried their Corporate Logos.

Many of the articles talk of increasing extremism, fundamentalism - of plain evil etc. – and the tear and the breaking up of The Society Fabric! 13 years later - The Truth arises – and what is most astonishing is that most of the things I had said and predicted then came to pass! And still as prevailing relevant too to date!

It was always my dream to redo the book on my own! Today that dream has become a reality! I hope you will enjoy reading the book again of past memories - a sense of Déjà Vu!

Despite strong temptations, I decided just to stick to make the book as best same as The Original version! I have used the book image of The Sequel book as front cover for this one – because honestly I did not like the previous one of boy whispering to boy – and thus an opportune time to redo it!

**Similar version is www.createspace.com/5041985**

**Tell me what you think!**

**Best wishes and regards,**

**Majid Al Suleimany**

## G.00      What They Said About My Books!

www.createspace.com/5026372 - www.createspace.com/5071159

www.createspace.com/5085322

## What They Said About My Books!

## All My Books Reviews & Accolades

## Books by Majid Al Suleimany

**Post my posting on my websites** – My Books Lukewarm Coverage in Media and Acceptance – it has become essential and my wish and desire to have in one place all my Books Reviews, Accolades, Comments, Independent Assessors and Evaluators – including those from Kindle – and from my First Book in 2003 to date – stretching over 12 years in total! Twelve Books in total – 3 in Road Safety – 3 in Arab Management and 6 assorted from my columns!

Also to act as a Quick Review of All My Works and as a Reference Research Point! If this will not work; nothing else will!

**Best wishes and regards,**

**Majid Al Suleimany - October 24, 2014**

**New Arab Management Book!**

**www.createspace.com/5083875**

## I.00        More Recent Comments Received!

- Dear Majid – May I order a copy of your lovely book? (Arab Management) – Dr. Faris Al Hajri
- Uncle – Do not forget we are not a Reading Nation! I was devastated when I found Borders was closing down! Then I asked myself – 51% of Omani population is under 21! Shook my head … to the brighter future? – Olav Mazroei
- Please communicate with Majid for the promotion of Road Safety Book Arabic/English at the scheduled event in Crowne Plaza Sohar on 28/11/2014 – Engineer Ahmed Al Mazrooei to his Secretary Memo
- **Also** – Many thanks for the dedication and local literature and whatever in the capacity of me and MAJIS will step in to support the initiative on Road Safety!

## November 8, 2014

You can go nowhere my Guru You are always in our heart Your books are our lights forever In Shaa Allah – **Mohamed Anwar Al Balushi**

Uncle Majid Insha Allah - Allah Will Bless you and Give you long life and health Ameen. Thank you for the link! – **Mohamed Al Nabhani**

### November 5, 2014

Majid, you have done a great job by writing so many books. This will be your priceless property! And the heritage you will leave not only for your family but for the whole Omani and the Arab Society.

**Seyyid Sakhawat Bukhari – FB – May 4 2014 - Tabinda Father!**

***

This is the world always! 5000 years ago the belly dancer used to earn more than the writer. . The drummer earns more than the Baker, carpenter* and black Smith. If u invite Einstein today for a science seminar and then invite a naked woman for a press conference, the public would leave Einstein and his science and gather around the naked woman. This is not our fault.  It is all because most of the people run after their fantasy and desires. Therefore they encourage the silly issues and run away from serious issues – **Dr. Mustafa Mahmoud**

**Posted by Olav Mazrui – Facebook**

***

Writing is a Passion of Writers, Authors and Columnists – and will not die even after the Author's death – because his works will always be there to be viewed and be read by future generations! As we have seen books still doing rounds by Authors long time gone centuries ago!

Thus those 'acting as God' to stop and prevent your writings are just deluding themselves more than anybody else! Just keep praying for them to return to the right path and ways – Ameen – Amen – and for Good Karma!

**For Bad Karma says** – Those who cause you hurt and pain – do not go for revenge – because God will let you watch as they 'screw up' in life! The East Africans also say – The man who goes up the ladder will come down sooner or later! Or as the Chinese say – if you are going to dig a grave for your enemy – dig two graves – and one keep for yourself!

Wish you luck and Take Care! – **Senior Public Official (Retired) - November 3, 2014**

You're right my dear, but they can never stop you from reaching the world! They don't know the real values of intellectuals, as the spinal cord of every civilization. Please let me know once you have the book here and which book store!! – **Dr. Faris Al Hajri**

## J.00        From The Newspaper!

**Fan (Omani)** – I think your reaction to the newspaper was to the point. My only advice is that don't allow the other party to get the best of you. Don't sound emotional. Just give them your piece of mind and move on...

**Lady Fan (Omani)**  - Well , its one's duty to speak up when things don't go well, if I were you I would have kept quiet cause its just like talking to a wall. It's not heard and nobody cares. It's just losing your face over and over again and nobody cares. I will never agree with you the way you humiliate yourself. You are a talented man you deserve the best of the respect. Be calm Majid it won't harm you and Allah sees everything. Be patient. If one door closes the other will open. Believe me.

**Fan (Omani)** - Spot on. I think there is a lot of hypocrisy in our society. You call a spade a spade and that's quite admirable. Very few people have the guts to go openly public in expressing a critical opinion. Did you get any response?

**From A Dr. Ph.D. – Dr. Faris Al Hajri - See Comments Here**

Dear Mr. Majid, We strongly support your endeavor. Remember, the best writers, noble people, celebrities, scientists, etc., were at first neglected by their own people; that is in West during the past centuries. But; today it all changed. So keep up, never give up, you're a very great writer, never let any negative people or pessimistic people put you down, the most you succeed, the more their feel ashamed of their wrong acts.

Finally, the Universe will respond to you abundantly. Keep up with those who are attracted by you, keep some distance to those who neglect you.

Keep looking at your achievements most whenever you get upset of a specific incident. You're great in the eyes of many who deserve to see your smiles. Cheers!!!

**Senior Omani Professional** – I admire your guts and in your sincerity to want to make changes in things before they go really bad!

**Some others 'too personal' to include here - but equally good (or have requested anonymity)!**

****

**As received.....**

**Sir - We are with you always!**

Yesterday night a group of us good getting together friends were having a meal at this Arabian Restaurant in Ghobrah and the subject starting moved to your columns articles. And your call about more Omanis to be needed represented in the especially English press and media as it is now being controlling and dominated by Indian people mainly and also some British peoples.

You also called for more stronger quality powering Omani Managers in the Press and media. Believe me Sir that people mistake us to be not knowing and not smart people and they can fool and play with us. But if they cannot learn than they will never learn in future. We are not stupid peoples. We aware and knowing too.

So Ustaadh please rest now. You have said it but they ignore you and not listen. You have done your job and duty as few Omanis that really care and feel. You take rest because you are now done and take rest Sir. Look after family only now.

Like you always tell us to take care! Ever admirer and fan to you Sir. We will never forget you till end of us.

**Please forgive my English. Omani (Young) Fan...**

****

Majid,

Two things.

1. Avoid criticising others unnecessarily. 2. Avoid GLORIFYING yourself excessively.

That is the secret of success.

****

Dear Ustaadh xxx and after compliments

In the name of Allah - With due respects Sir -

A friend had forwarded me the not necessary response that this guy YYYYY has sent to Ami Majid. Unfortunately, people miss the very important thing that this man is highly appreciated and followed by many young Omanis as one lone voice that really cares and feels for us!

He is one of the few that took great risks and dangers to himself even harm when even in PDO and he suffered a lot life later on because of his stand on things and everyone.

It is very sad and tragic that you his so-called friends treat him like this and I can only assume an element of jealousy and envy - perhaps because of his popularity. You have hurt him so much and now he has decided to stop writing his websites and columns.

Only time will tell the repercussions in the future and please accept my sincere apologies for this email. Forgive my English also Sir.

Allah protect and preserve our country from all things bad inside and outside Ameen - Unquote!

### B        Response verbatim from Number Two Responder - Quote

*Dear Majid*

*If you want my personal advice and sent in good faith please keep away from all these people ex PDO especially because you cannot remove the hypocrisies and double standards within them.*

*It will not surprise me and from seeing some of the names that they will be communicating to each other and laughing and sneering you behind your back. This is how they are and will always be! Some of them even got later in life great personal tragedies and woes in their lives and in their families but they will never learn!*

*Keep away from them and even stop writing even. This is a lost cause beyond redemption and only time will tell! So please keep away! All of them combined cannot even be 20% of what you are as Majid.*

*I will always pray for you and your family Amin*

**Unquote.**

**And finally to those that finally killed my columns - I said to them -**

**Quote -**

*I see that ZZZ (expatriate person) has now taken over my columns! It will not surprise me that you will be paying him even 3 or 4 times my rate - but that is how things are nowadays! So it is not surprising to me at all. Take care and all the best!*
**- Unquote!**

**Now you know why I am giving writing in this website low priority from now onwards! It was good whilst it lasted - but everything 9good) has to end one day!**

**\*\*\*\***

**ALL ABOUT MY BOOKS! ALL THE BOOKS REVIEWS!**

BOOKS BY MAJID AL SULEIMANY

MAJID AL SULEIMANY

**www.createspace.com/5071159**

## K.00        From A Top VIP!

After Compliments

Dear Ustaadh Majid;

Thank you about the information about your new Road Safety book Arabic – Behind The Wheel!

- **www.createspace.com/4875352**  خلف عجلة القيادة

I would like to express my appreciation of your kind efforts to deliver to my office your two Arab Management books – Psychology of Arab Management Thinking! - **www.trafford.com/08-0889** - and **A Cry For Help!**

**http://bookstore.trafford.com/Products/SKU-000142695/A-Cry-For-Help.aspx**

.

More importantly for writing these books and letting the rest of us in the country and the world the issues and aspects that have been troubling you for such a long time and your feelings that you needed to write these books as information to the rest and detailing your own personal experiences and exposures over 35 years and most of it being in PDO of 25 years services and as a Human Resources Management Consultant for later years.

I am pleased to inform you that I have now read both the books and am lost in words of where to start, pause or end! You have done a brilliant work and your efforts need to be recommended and to be appreciated.

I have recommended your books to my colleagues as Essential Reading for us in The Leadership. I personally think this far outweighs any monetary and other awards that you may have received so far.

My Congratulations and Thanks once again. Please let me know if you are writing any sequels and when The Road Safety Book will be available locally in Oman.

Please accept best regards and wishes

## L.00    My New Books

## L.01        Arab Management: Reality or Myth?
## The Arab Manager!

ARAB MANAGEMENT: REALITY OR MYTH? THE ARAB MANAGER!

ARAB MANAGEMENT: REALITY OR MYTH?
THE ARAB MANAGER!

Context and Perspectives - Arabian Management Services
By Majid Al Suleimany MBA
www.myownmajid.com

MAJID AL SULEIMANY

www.createspace.com/4960056
**Why I Wrote This Book!**

- *Do not tell me you are going to write this book! I just cannot believe it!* – **British CEO**
- *I thought after your last book – and the end of your columns – you will stop writing! You have me pleasantly surprised!* – **Senior Omani Public Official (Retired)**

This is my Third Arab Management Book after *Psychology of Arab Management Thinking!* And *A Cry For Help!* And my 12th book! Three books are on Road Safety and the balance are based on my columns and writings!

The book focuses on what is particular about the type of local Arab Management, its context and perspectives, and what is peculiar, special, or particular to that work in the context and in comparison to the Management Styles of other nations. Using personal experiences, examples, and illustrations, Al Suleimany exposes the new reality and truth and moves away from the trend and approach of hiding issues and problems. The books are soul searching, in deep self-analysis and critical evaluation of one's own people in the field.

The Author extols the culture and importance of work in his religion and the pitfalls and lackluster attitude of some of the Managers in position about the Accountabilities, Principles, Transparencies, Professionalism and Ethics of Management – and vis-à-vis their roles, aspects and responsibilities.

The Arab countries are far richer with abundant reserves and more importantly with a healthy and young population. In spite of all these why do we lag behind others in many spheres? Is there anything wrong with the Arab Management? He says, "He is baffled and confused".

"As Arabs, work is worshipped as if it is in praying. Arabs are also brought up to be polite, courteous and decent (at least a majority of us). Abrupt, ugly, rudeness and distort are discouraged. Also it is not easy to say NO – as part of the culture, customs, traditions and heritage. So what went wrong here – especially in management circles? Why are we behind the rest of the world, despite all our riches and resources?"

The Gulf Cooperation Council countries are some of the richest ones in the world.

Despite the Middle East holding huge gas and oil reserves of the world, very little is known about the area, in particular about Arabian Management aspects.

All my Arab Management books have been written after a major upheaval in my life at the work front and elsewhere involving my life!  I was always under the impression that my book A Cry For Help! As was going to be my last book in Arab Management with the events that followed proving my case why 'I needed help!' as an Arab Manager! Though trying best to keep to myself – and trying to avoid conflict and confrontations as much as I possibly could – but people would not leave me alone! They were still after me!

## L. 02.    It Is All About Driving!

## My Books on Road Safety (Three)

## By Majid Al Suleimany

September 1, 2014

**www.createspace.com/4875352**

خلف عجلة القيادة

أن تكون سائقًا آمنًا

ماجد السليماني

www.createspace.com/4875352

www.bethesafedriver.com - www.myownmajid.com
www.myown-ebooks.com

- أُخِذت بقراءة الكتاب، حتى إنني أعدت التفكير في ما اعتقدت أني كنت أعرفه عن السلامة على الطريق. رئيس تنفيذي لشركة بريطانية

- تأثرت كثيرًا بما ورد من قصص مأساوية مرعبة في الكتاب. مدير عام عماني

تشير الإحصائيات إلى أن سلطنة عمان من بين البلدان التي تشهد أعلى عدد من الحوادث المرورية والإصابات الناجمة عنها على مستوى العالم. ومع انتشار السلوكيات المتهورة في قيادة السيارات فإنه من الأهمية بمكان البدء في تغيير الثقافة السائدة في استخدام الطرق. يقدم هذا الكتاب الجديد والرائد البراهين الدالَّة على أهمية التزام قواعد السلامة أثناء قيادة المركبة. يحفل الكتاب بالعديد من القصص المؤلمة والمؤثرة مُبيّنًا مخاطر الطريق والثمن الباهظ الذي يدفعه السائق جرّاء تقصيره. ومع تأكيد كبار المسؤولين على أهمية السلامة على الطريق، آن الأوان ليكون سائقو المركبات أكثر حذرًا في القيادة. إن هذا الكتاب القيّم؛ "أن تكون سائقًا آمنًا! خلف عجلة القيادة! سرد جديد عن السلامة على الطريق" من شأنه أن ينقذ حياة الكثيرين في أنحاء البلاد.

يفتح هذا الكتاب أعيننا على أهمية السلامة على الطريق والقيادة الآمنة، وذلك من خلال مجموعة من القصص الواقعية يسردها ضحايا الحوادث المرورية الذين يرغبون بنقل تجاربهم للآخرين ومشاركتهم الدروس والعبر لتثقيف سائقي السيارات في كل مكان في الوطن. يجدر بكل من يمسك بعجلة القيادة أن يقرأ هذا الكتاب الذي لا يُقدّر بثمن ويمكنه أن ينقذ الكثيرين. مستلهمًا الحادث المروّع الذي ألمّ بعائلة زميل لنا في العمل يسعى الكتاب إلى تشجيع القيادة الآمنة حول العالم. ويأمل الكتاب من خلال سرد قصص الحوادث المرورية والخسائر الناجمة عنها أن يلقى صداه لدى القُرّاء. إن القيادة المتهورة دائمًا لها عواقبها سواء نتجت عن الحادث إصابات أو خسائر في الأرواح أو الممتلكات أو حتى صدمات نفسية. يمنح هذا الكتاب قُرّاءه الأسباب المقنعة ليكونوا سائقين آمنين.

يُشاد بهذا الكتاب باعتباره من أهم الكتب التي صدرت هذا العام، ويُتوقّع أن يكون له تأثير كبير.

سيكون هذا الكتاب هو الكتاب الذي تنتظره الدولة ويباركه أهم الشخصيات في المجتمع بدءًا من حضرة صاحب الجلالة السلطان قابوس بن سعيد المعظم، حفظه الله ورعاه، إلى سماحة الشيخ أحمد بن حمد الخليلي، المفتي العام للسلطنة. وبأهدافه النبيلة وطرقه الفعّالة يهدف هذا الكتاب إلى إحداث نقلة نوعية في حياة كل سائق.

**نص الغلاف الخلفي**

تشير الإحصائيات إلى أن سلطنة عمان من بين البلدان التي تشهد أعلى عدد من الحوادث المرورية والإصابات الناجمة عنها على مستوى العالم. ومع انتشار السلوكيات المتهورة في قيادة السيارات فإنه من الأهمية بمكان البدء في تغيير الثقافة السائدة في استخدام الطرق. يقدم هذا الكتاب الجديد والرائد البراهين الدالّة على أهمية الالتزام بقواعد السلامة أثناء قيادة المركبة.

يحفل الكتاب بالعديد من القصص المؤلمة والمؤثرة مُبيّنًا مخاطر الطريق والثمن الباهظ الذي يدفعه السائق جرّاء تقصيره. ومع تأكيد كبار المسؤولين على أهمية السلامة على الطريق، آن الأوان ليكون سائقو المركبات أكثر حذرًا في القيادة. إن هذا الكتاب القيّم؛ "أن تكون سائقًا آمنًا! خلف عجلة القيادة! سرد جديد عن السلامة على الطريق" من شأنه أن ينقذ حياة الكثيرين في أنحاء البلاد.

يفتح هذا الكتاب أعيننا على أهمية السلامة على الطريق والقيادة الآمنة، وذلك من خلال مجموعة من القصص الواقعية يسردها ضحايا الحوادث المرورية الذين يرغبون بنقل تجاربهم للآخرين ومشاركتهم الدروس والعبر لتثقيف سائقي السيارات في كل مكان في الوطن. يجدر بكل من يمسك بعجلة القيادة أن يقرأ هذا الكتاب الذي لا يُقدّر بثمن ويمكنه أن ينقذ الكثيرين.

مستلهمًا الحادث المروّع الذي ألمّ بعائلة زميل لنا في العمل يسعى الكتاب إلى تشجيع القيادة الآمنة حول العالم. ويأمل الكتاب من خلال سرد قصص الحوادث المرورية والخسائر الناجمة عنها أن يلقى صداه لدى القُرّاء. إن القيادة المتهورة دائمًا لها عواقبها سواء نتجت عن الحادث إصابات أو خسائر في الأرواح أو الممتلكات أو حتى صدمات نفسية. يمنح هذا الكتاب قُرّاءه الأسباب المقنعة ليكونوا سائقين آمنين.

## الكتابـ هل كلّه عن قيادة السيارات!
يقوم الكتاب على قصص واقعية حول الحوادث المرورية وضحاياها؛ وأثرها على حياتهم وحياة عائلاتهم من حولهم، والعبر والدروس التي يتعلّمها الآخرون من هذه القصص.

لو أن حادثًا مروريًا واحدًا أمكن تجنّبه بقراءة هذا الكتاب، فإن المقصد منه سيتحقّق!

***

# خلف عجلة القيادة
### أن تكون سائقًا آمِنًا
## ماجد السليماني

## L.03      Arabic – Behind The Wheel! Being The Safe Driver!

## By Majid Al Suleimany

- Gripping read that made me rethink what I thought I knew on Road Safety Awareness! – **British CEO**

- Touched my heart with such rending tragic horrifying stories! – **Omani GM**

The Sultanate of Oman has one of the highest numbers of automobile accidents and casualties in the world. With such rampant and reckless automobile behaviors on the rise, there has never been a better time to change the culture and safety of our roads. With this groundbreaking new book, drivers across the nation will finally have proof in hand as to why they should drive safer.

Filled with heartbreaking and emotional true stories, this illuminating book shows drivers everywhere the dangers of the road and the true cost of negligence. With high-ranking officials across the country acknowledging the importance of road safety, it is time for drivers everywhere to be more careful and drive safer. An invaluable road safety tool! *Behind the Wheel, Being the Safe Driver! New Road Safety Book* can save lives all across the country.

This eye-opening book emphasizes the importance of road safety and careful driving through a collection of real-life stories from accident victims who share the hard experiences and lessons they learned in order to better educate drivers everywhere. A vital read for anyone behind the wheel, this priceless book has the ability to save lives!

Inspired by a horrific crash which took the lives of a coworker's family - *Being the Safe Driver! Behind The Wheel!* - strives to encourage safer driving across the world. Filled with dramatic, true stories of accidents and loss, the book's poignant moments are sure to resonate with all readers.

Whether an accident results in injury, property loss, or simply a shaken emotional self, reckless driving always has consequences. From horrible injuries to destroyed families, this enlightening book does a fantastic job of giving all readers reasons to become safe drivers.

**www.bethesafedriver.com – www.myownmajid.com**

**\*\*\***

**For Direct Ordering**

**www.createspace.com/4875352**

**\*\*\*\***

## L.04        The English Books Versions!

## For Direct Ordering!

**Behind The Wheel!**        – www.createspace.com/4655681

**Being The Safe Driver!**    - www.createspace.com/4097374

## M        My Arab Psychology Book Wins
## US Golden Seal Award!

### www.trafford.com/08-0889
### The US Review of Books!

*It is from the womb of art that criticism was born! – **Charles Baudelaire***

The US Review of Books connects worldwide Authors and Publishers with Professional Reviewers. It is an independent free running body – and the books and Reviewers are chosen at random order.

My books USA Trafford Publishers sent me this note – which is very good news on my Arab Management book – Psychology of Arab Management Thinking! – Context and Perspectives. My book had won The Golden Seal Award – and is shortlisted for the prestigious Eric Hoffer Award.

See The Golden Seal Stamp on The New Cover – plus Write up back cover by them!

The mere fact it reached this stage – and competed against books from well-known world Authors and Writers – and some of them being great Researchers, Professors and great Literary Artists is an achievement in itself – as it was my first Arab Management book! More information at **www.myownmajid.com** – I am pleased to share with you on our success!

## B    The Book Review

**The book was reviewed by one John E. Roper – USA – Quote –**

**www.theusreview.com/reviews/Psychology-Suleimany.html**

**www.trafford.com/08-0889**

*"It is only by building on existing strengths, and moving forwards on established capabilities that economic maturity can be achieved and rising living standards maintained."*

Writers approach their craft with a variety of motivations. Some search for fame, others for fortune, and still others because spinning words together is one of the few things they are really good at. Some, though, write because what they have to say is burning inside them, and the only release is to share with others what has so inflamed their emotions. Such is the case with the author, whose passion for his people and his culture has driven him to speak out against the problems within Arab management practices so that, as he says, he can one day tell his grandchildren that by writing books he did something about them.

The author approaches his topic as an insider. Having worked extensively in the global business environment and in human resources in particular, both with Arab and international leadership, he has seen firsthand the shortsightedness, prejudice, paranoia, and autocratic tendencies of many Arab managers as well as the unfortunate fact that motivation and morale are frequently higher among Arab employees when someone other than one of their own countrymen is in charge. These observations have gnawed at him, and he questions not only why the situation within the corporate world is like this but also what can be done about it.

As an Omani, the Author offers great insight into his own country's management issues, but he is quick to point out that many of the observations he makes can be applied to businesses throughout the Arab world. While the subject matter of this book will mainly appeal to readers approaching it from an Arab perspective, students of international business can also learn a lot from the author's research –

**Unquote**

**Above - Image – Front Cover**

**www.trafford.com/08-0889**

## C      What The Book Had Said!

As aforementioned, the book is about Arab Management issues and aspects – with personal experiences, exposures and examples of the Author stretching over 35 years experiences in Management and Human Resources – and as a Consultant, Advisor and Expert for over the past 10 years in a number of companies.

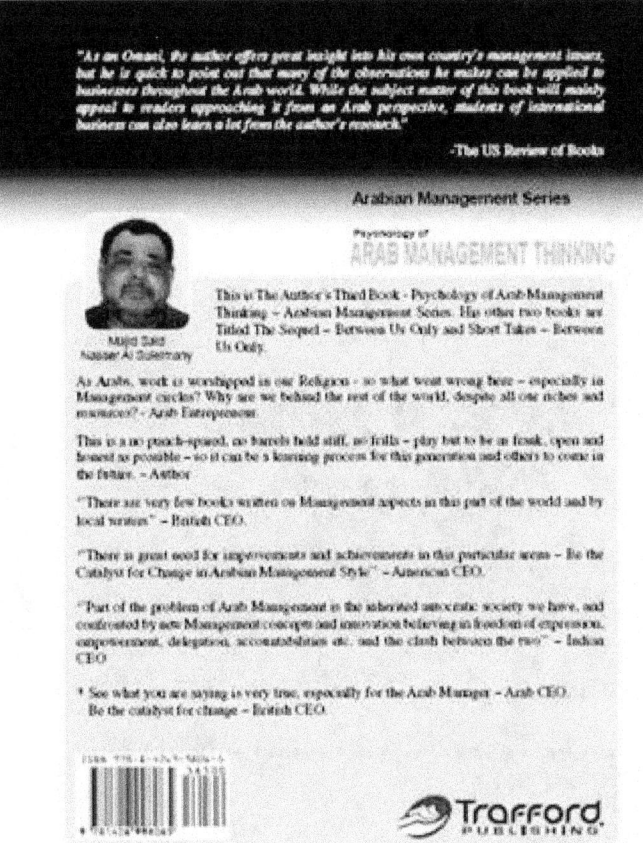

**Image Back Cover**

**www.trafford.com/08-0889**

**Book Theme** – This is a no punch spared, no barrels held, no frills and no play stuff book but to be as open, frank, sincere and honest as far as is possible – in deep soul search and self-analysis – so it can be a learning process for this generation – and for others to come in the future.

**Continued – Author's Note** – For a long time now, I have been putting off the idea of writing this book – though it had been on my mind for a long time now. The mere idea of writing this book scared me to bits and pieces – for many valid and pertinent reasons.

As Arabs, work is worshipped (Islamic Religion calls on us to respect work like as if it is in praying!). We are also brought up to be polite, courteous and decent (at least a majority of us). Abrupt, ugly, rudeness and distort are discouraged. Also it is not easy to say NO – as part of the culture, customs, traditions and heritage. So what went wrong here – especially in Management circles? Why are we behind the rest of the world, despite all our riches and resources?

I hope you will enjoy the book. I have tried to be as frank, open, forthright, honest, sincere and genuine as I can – as Readers who know me can give credence and credibility to me and will vouch and authenticate my works.

**I have not spared myself, so there is just for it to be honest, sincere, genuine and hard hitting – sparing no one. Just No One!**

**Take Care!**

**By Majid Al Suleimany**

**June 18th 2013**

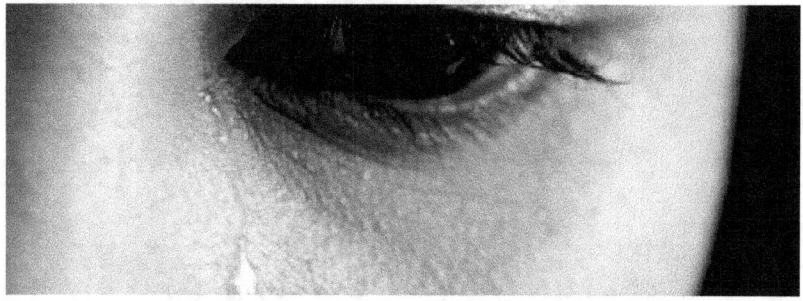

**Image Tears – www.myown-ebooks.com**

## N   Bird's Eye View!
## More Comments Remembered!

- Please do not stop writing! Writing is our blood and our life line – and Writers only stop if they die!  - When I wanted to stop writing last time! - The Features Editor
- The (UK) University is very much impressed by your writing! We did not realise that such talents existed in your part of the world! We invite you to look at our Doctorate programmes and let us know what we can do for you!
- We recommend you translate your works into Arabic to reach the wider Arabic world – Tunisian University Professor
- It is disappointing about your remarks that your society does not appreciate and value your writings! We invite you to consider to move over to USA where definitely your writings are appreciated! It will be easy to get a Green Card with your qualifications and achievements! – The USA Lady Publisher!
- I was very sad to read your article – and to see the things that are happening to you! I wish you were Turkish and could write in Turkish! – Turkish Lady Fan
- I went to The Frankfurt International Book Fair – but was very much disappointed not to find any of your books there! What is happening! – Lady Fan in Germany
- Added Comments – It happens even here in Local Books Exhibitions!
- And so many others – can fill pages and pages!
- Look at my Facebook, Twitter and Linkedin Pages – and see the Followers!
- Better to End Now!

# O    My Epitaph!

## I want to be remembered!

November 24, 2012

## Majid Epitaph (Legacy) – I want to be remembered!

A long time ago as a kid, I used to hear people talk about death and how they will go! I always wondered out aloud how I would go – if my turn came up next!

I always prayed that I would go sudden and people surprised he went away that fast! But I never want to cause trouble and inconveniences to others before I die – if I was to choose these things! But it is all in God Allah hands!

Anyway, I had this dream of 'dying by starvation' – I do not know what it meant! Was it going to be real as in the dream – or as a metaphor like liking to eat too much and getting fatter by day – and as now being diabetic case?

Or would it be like my late Father PBUH where he wanted food and water but was denied by The Doctors (they were using instead drips!) – because they needed to operate on his stomach – because there was a blockage in his small intestines – and till after the operation could be given food!

Anyway only God Allah SWT Knows these things best!

**Sorry for a morbid subject!**

Here lies a person who in all his life had acted and stood up for the rights of others – and to whatever extent and even harm and injury and damage to himself personally – and he went down that way!

Where he could change things himself he did – otherwise he spoke out for Change. Always wanted to be fair, just, professional, principled, correct and ethical in all things he did.

A person who was always sincere, genuine and honest – frank, open and forthright who always looked at The Bigger Picture – and never wanted things to go wrong as his focus and theme in life! Even though many of his efforts were never acknowledged, accepted and realized – and he became a victim himself in his life, career, and future and with his family too!

**He wants to be remembered that way only!**

**Please Pray for Him – when they tell you he is gone!**

### Majid Said Nasser Al Suleimany

### The Author –

### November 24, 2012

### This is me!

# Goodbye; Between Us Only!

# They Will Not Publish This!

## By Majid Al Suleimany

My Books Websites –

www.myownmajid.com

www.myown-ebooks.com

www.majidbooks.com

My Columns

www.majidwritecom

www.majidall.com

November 29, 2014

Thanks For Buying / Reading This Book!

Best Wishes and Regards,

Majid Al Suleimany

# BOOK END!

www.ingramcontent.com/pod-product-compliance
Lightning Source LLC
Chambersburg PA
CBHW051957280526
45793CB00005B/748